The Stakeholders' Golden Rule

The Unholy Trinity of Politics, Stupidity and Dereliction
All in the Best Interest of the People of Texas

Raymond A. Giuliani Jr.

This book is a work of commentary based on my time at ERCOT. As
such, this book reflects my views and opinions on how the quasi-governmental structure of ERCOT and resulting lack of fiduciary accountability enabled bad behavior to adversely affect
work being done on behalf of the people of Texas. All quotations
in this book reflect my best recollection of the essence of the conversations and may not be verbatim quotations, unless a specific
source is cited. At times, I have taken creative license for purposes
of clarity and readability.

Contents

DERELICTION

CONFIDENT IGNORANCE

EPILOGUE

Acknowledgments

To Dan Wright, who took a chance on a first-time author. You convinced me to stop trying to disguise my feelings in a fictitious novel and just tell my story. It was all I really wanted to do. Your hybrid approach to publishing worked perfectly for me. You are a valued business partner and an even better friend.

To my editor, Mike Towle, who told me to quit beating around the bush and just come out with it! You are an elite accomplished writer in your own right. Thank you for helping me.

To my son, Ray III, my daughters, Meredith and Emily—I am very proud of you. You are precisely what every baby boomer was looking for in the next generation. Thank you for your help in keeping this book on track and not sounding too much like sour grapes spouting from an old man. Love you.

To my wife, Sue. My sunshine. I hope you don't mind sharing parts of our wonderful life through chapters in this book. You are my inspiration to try to make every day the best day ever. With you, my future is always full of anticipation of fun and joy. I love you so very much.

And to the people of ERCOT who worked both for and with me, this book is dedicated to your creativity, fearlessness of taking a risk, attention to detail, hard work, and daily focus and enthusiasm to build something unique for others to emulate worldwide. I was so lucky to be asked to nurture your talents and to learn from you.

Preface

This is a story about my five-plus years at The Electric Reliability Council of Texas—known as ERCOT. ERCOT is a membership-based nonprofit corporation that was tasked in the late 1990s by the Texas legislature with enabling the deregulation of Texas investor-owned electric utilities. Its responsibilities were the centerpiece of a magnificent new governmental undertaking to make electricity a wholesale and retail market commodity.

The members of ERCOT called themselves "stakeholders." They consisted of consumers, incumbent investor-owned utility generators, independent generators, power marketers, retail electric providers, transmission and distribution providers, cooperatives, and municipally owned electric utilities—in other words, everyone with a "stake" in the electric power business, from supply through demand.

When I joined ERCOT in 2002, it was still suffering growing pains. My story focuses on a period in that evolution that proved to be quite painful for all who were trying to fulfill the goals of their stakeholder group. For me, it was a period where truth became stranger than fiction. It was a period dominated by politics and ethics.

Politics and ethics are manmade creations. They are products of the human spirit, and, as an integral part of our nature, they have no defined structure. Countless variables make up any one of the seemingly infinite number of political or ethical outcomes.

It confounds the mind when we realize how our world is driven by such inexact concepts. Religions, governments, corporations, and even informal groups of people are at their mercy. People try to control them with an array of constraints—from fuzzy guidelines to strict sets of rules.

Some people believe that ethics should control politics. To them, it establishes the obvious boundaries for political activities. It is the foundational concept for religions. And, perhaps surprising to some people, investor-owned corporations, often seen as having no ethical boundaries, are in fact bound by the ethical concept of fiduciary responsibility to act in the best interest of the company's customers and its owners.

The foundational ethical concept for governments is a maze of political procedures of checks and balances. Unfortunately, or fortunately, depending on your point of view, politics is the only control over the ethics associated with overall government spending. Unlike corporate America, there are typically no prescribed fiduciary responsibilities to constituents or taxpayers.

In fact, governments often choose to ignore any notion of financial accountability that might impede their effort to optimize the greater good. That concept manifested itself at ERCOT as the "Stakeholders' Golden Rule." It enabled a seemingly bottomless pit of opportunity for fraud and financial dereliction and challenged my professional compass every day during that critical period in ERCOT's evolution.

It's a safe bet that you have both witnessed and been involved directly in similar real-life experiences associated with politics, ethics, and the greater good. They stretched your patience and ruined many days. You can't ignore it. But you should keep it separate from your family and always be at peace with the reflection you see when you look in a mirror.

I hope you find my book to be entertaining and enlightening as we try to make our world better.

1
Daydream

The lights were dim. Little snack bowls sat on the end tables. Each of us had a small cup of red punch. The smell of perfume was calming yet exciting. Sixties music played on the record player atop the chest along the side wall. It was Betty Everett singing "The Shoop Shoop Song (It's in His Kiss)." I had heard that song many times, but, for some reason, in this setting, it made me really nervous.

It was prearranged that our hostess's parents would stay in the back room. There was respect for our privacy without sacrificing safety. All part of a well-thought-out plan. It was time, but for what I wasn't sure. The girls had discussed the details weeks earlier. They needed to take charge.

Perspiration was on the boys' faces. I thought it was a little warm in the room. It wasn't. Our sweat was from anticipation and uncomfortable new clothes. No telling what these girls were up to. All of us had turned fourteen within the previous few months. We felt our bodies changing in a new way as we sat in the circle.

The girls knew exactly what they were doing. The boys didn't have a clue.

Janet was my first date. She had asked me to the party. It was weird. I expected to answer her with my usual no but for some reason I said yes. It must have been the new chemical reactions going on in my brain. Of course, my mom thought it was cute.

"You'll have fun," she said. "You'll see."

How could I have fun? The collar of my new shirt was irritating my neck. I hated wearing pants with a belt. And my new shoes were too tight.

Janet was attractive. She looked more like a young woman than a girl who had just turned fourteen. She had the most beautiful blue eyes. Lily-white skin—clearly of German descent. Slightly taller than I was, she wore flat shoes to keep me from being uncomfortable. At fourteen, many Italian-American boys, like me, began to suffer from height envy. My grandmother told me that we made up for it with our passion for life. I didn't know Janet was going to put me to the test.

We all sat in a circle. The girls smiled confidently. The boys smiled, too, but that was from tension. More than half of us wore braces. Fortunately, the dim lighting kept our braces from detracting from the mood. Janet and I had full sets—a little reminder of the childhood we were about to leave behind. Our hostess, Jill, spun the bottle. It pointed at Janet. It was her turn to choose. Of course, she chose me.

Janet held my hand and led me toward a closet. It was dark. I had no idea what to do. It didn't matter. Janet was taking me to school. She knew it—and was deliberate in her delivery of Lesson

No. 1. The reality of being so close to her made me both nervous and happy. I felt myself shaking a little bit. I couldn't stop it. It didn't matter. Janet was in charge. She held me gently but firmly. She knew precisely what to do. I calmed down and got in sync with her mood.

The smell of her perfume was intoxicating. Her blue eyes sparkled, even in the dark. Her body was perfect. Her waist was thin and easy to hug. I became aware of the meaning of *perky*. Her buttocks were round and soft. She quivered as I moved my hands down to them, then she pressed her body closer. I was still a little lost. Not to worry, she was in charge. Our first kiss was a little awkward with the braces and the attached rubber bands getting in the way. Neither one of us, though, let the braces and rubber bands remind us that we were only fourteen. She tasted so good as she stuck her tongue into my mouth, massaging my palate.

She pressed hard against me to feel my excitement. The lesson was beginning to make sense to me. The next steps came naturally. She rubbed against me, signaling to me her increasing desire . . .

The sound of a loud siren burst my bubble. Bright lights were flashing behind me. I looked down at the speedometer. I was going eighty-five.

The sixties music blaring from my car radio had triggered a daydream.

I needed to get back to reality, so I turned off the radio and pulled out my license and registration. I knew the drill. I'd give it my best shot to try to leave with just a warning.

2
Painting Reality

I was on my way to Austin and headed for a new job, a new adventure. It was my first drive to Austin. Sue was still in Atlanta and would fly out to meet me in a few days. The long, straight Texas highway seemed to have no end. If I didn't know better, I would swear that the world was flat. There were also many cows, but the longhorn steers were what caught my eye. I hadn't seen a live, longhorn steer up close since my last trip from Atlanta to El Paso thirty years earlier.

It was November 2002, and the scenery was a bit boring. I thought about the coming spring when the famous Texas wildflowers would be in full bloom. I imagined field after field of bluebonnets, Drummond phlox and Indian blanket creating patches of blue, red, yellow, pink, and white. A few towns along the way would have helped slow me down, but I hadn't passed one since I left the interstate.

While listening to my favorite music, with no traffic or curves in the road, I fell into a daydream of thirty-seven years ago. It was an innocent mistake.

The bright lights flashed in my rearview mirror. I pulled over to the side of the road. The trooper got out of the car. The wide-brimmed hat made me think this might be a Texas Ranger looking for something more than a speeder. I had heard stories about them. This wasn't going to be easy. Sharing my daydream with him would cause more harm than good.

Then I realized I might have a chance. It was only a Texas state trooper, not a Texas Ranger, and the trooper was a woman. She might love my story. I figured I had at least half a chance at painting a picture of my daydream that she might find compelling enough to let me go with only a stern "Slow it down, sir."

The road sign next to my stopped car indicated I was in La Grange. I had heard of it. It was the setting of the play and the movie *The Best Little Whorehouse in Texas*, featuring its Texas Chicken Ranch. In that play, Miss Wulla Jean expected and accepted a little bending of the rules. Perhaps it was fate, and maybe I could talk my way out of a speeding ticket.

The trooper carefully approached my car. Mid-thirties, I guessed. Good-looking with a large bosom filling her uniform. Maybe she worked at the Chicken Ranch at night. I made an extra effort to avoid any such jokes. Her last name was Farrell.

She wanted my license and registration and returned to her car. I wished she would turn off those annoying blinking lights. There was no one else within sight of us. And I hardly represented criminal activity.

After determining I wasn't a fugitive from justice, Trooper Farrell returned to my car. She said she pulled me over because I was speeding and weaving. Next, she asked me to get out of my car and open the trunk. I assumed that my out-of-state Georgia license plate put her in extra-care mode. I told her that I wasn't transporting any drugs or firearms. She believed me. My suitcases and briefcase appeared legitimate enough. I closed the trunk.

She asked me where I was going. I told her that I was headed to Austin to begin a new job. Then she looked me in the eye and asked if I was drinking or doing drugs. I said, "No, but can I tell you what happened?" I hoped she would understand my rationale for exceeding the speed limit.

As is always the case, perception is reality. People's perceptions are shaped by the pictures painted for them. This was an opportunity to share with her a bit of my artistic talent. There is typically a standard deviation from the truth in any such painting. It is my nature to take an extra step to minimize any deviation.

Could I convince her to go lightly? I would simply be honest with Trooper Farrell.

I told her that the vastness and beauty of the Texas countryside made me too comfortable at the wheel. I shared my daydream with her, hoping to strike a sympathetic chord. The retro music. It was all about innocence. It was about growing up. I told her about the party. I told her about the beautiful girl who took me to school. The daydream had no business interfering with my safety on the highway. I was really sorry about that.

To my surprise, Trooper Farrell was intrigued with my first romantic encounter. She laughed at my reference about being taken to school. We agreed that girls matured a lot faster than boys. It must have reminded her of something similar in her early teens. It looked like I had a pretty good shot to avoid a ticket. Her body language showed that her guard was down. She was feeling more like a sensitive human being than a stuffy Texas state trooper.

Then it happened. She asked what became of my relationship with that sweet fourteen-year-old girl. I told Trooper Farrell that I ignored her after that night. I never talked to her at school despite the tears in her eyes each time I saw her. My reason was that I wasn't sure I wanted to marry her, so the best way to avoid complications was to cut it off.

I felt obligated to give Trooper Farrell an accurate account of subsequent events. The only picture I was comfortable painting was of what really took place.

My newfound Texas state trooper friend began to show signs of transforming back into her role as a stuffy cop. She folded her arms in front of her. Her smile disappeared. That was it. Trooper Farrell didn't like my story. She abruptly gave me a speeding ticket. After reciting the script related to the ticket, she said, "Welcome to Texas, Mr. Giuliani."

It wasn't the first time my big mouth bit me in the ass. I knew it wouldn't be the last time, either. I was always compelled to give much more information than necessary to ensure that I communicated a complete painting of the truth. Some called it brutal honesty. My former business colleagues referred to it as my big mouth.

I was unaware of the treasure trove of artists I was about to meet in my new job at the entity overseeing the entire Texas electricity grid and the recently deregulated $30 billion electricity market. I would find out that the inherent nature of a number of them was the opposite of mine. They only painted pictures of the false reality they wanted others to see. You probably know them better as backstabbers and swindlers. It was time to engage that large group of artists in the arena known as The Electric Reliability Council of Texas.

POLITICS

3
Perspective

The Electric Reliability Council of Texas (ERCOT) was a membership-based nonprofit corporation that was tasked in the late 1990s by the Texas legislature with enabling the deregulation of Texas investor-owned electric utilities. Its responsibilities were the centerpiece of a magnificent new governmental undertaking to make electricity a wholesale and retail market commodity.

When I arrived at ERCOT in 2002, it was still suffering growing pains. It had lost its leader—ENRON. Deregulation of the electric utility industry was a brainchild of ENRON. The new structure of the industry and, most importantly, the governance of ERCOT was a product of ENRON ingenuity. ENRON had crumbled due to its obsession with pushing the envelope of business ethics. Its alleged innovative financing techniques that drove seemingly endless capital spending and its disdain of business ethical constraints brought it to a devastating end. The ghost of ENRON haunted me from my initial job interview with ERCOT to my last day there.

The headquarters for The Electric Reliability Council of Texas was in Austin. About thirty-five miles northeast was the town of Taylor, the location for a new ERCOT operations facility. A beautiful new all-brick-and-stone building, it was built to meet the requirements of a statewide electric grid operator. It was constructed to survive any bad weather condition, including up to a category F4 tornado. The operations facility at our headquarters in Austin would continue to operate as usual, but as a redundant backup to the new primary operation in Taylor.

Taylor was a rural Texas town, a living reminder of early 1950s Americana. It was like a Hollywood movie set, only real. When I arrived, Taylor was actually being used as the background for a new movie. I found out that the people there were accustomed to such events. The film industry had tagged Taylor as being rich in scenic backdrops. Some recent popular movies had been filmed at various local spots. *The Rookie* and *Friday Night Lights* were shot, at least in part, in and around Taylor.

Barbecued brisket seemed to be the primary source of nutrition, served on either paper plates or wax paper. No franchises, just family-run dives with screened-door entrances, old wooden furniture, low overhead, and high-quality food. The brisket was a little too tough for me. I preferred the pulled pork and sausage. When you left the establishment, it would be clear where you had eaten. The scent in your clothes gave you away. Even your hair smelled like barbecue.

The day after my arrival, the new ERCOT facility opened. Key Texas legislative leaders, public utility commissioners and their staff, and a number of industry executives came to Taylor for the dedication of the new building. They gathered in the front court-yard area under the hot Texas sun.

Deregulation of the electric utility business in Texas was a game changer. It spawned new companies in the supply chain from electric generation to consumption. The incumbent electric utilities were gone. Their businesses had to be split into separate companies: generation, transmission and distribution, and retail electric provider. The result was a brave new world of electricity competition affecting everybody. The success of ERCOT was inex-tricably intertwined with the success of deregulation in Texas. It was a big deal. The picture I had in my mind's eye was the chart on the next page.

I used it quite often as a reference.

I was the new vice president and chief of market opera-tions. All of the current officers were at the dedication. They had guided ERCOT from its infancy. They were enjoying the celebra-tion of their hard work to complete the construction of the new 85,000-square-foot building, which would give ERCOT the phys-ical facilities it needed for a state-of-the art grid operations cen-ter and additional office space. In fact, we still would not have enough office space. ERCOT had obtained enough land at the same Taylor location to build a second facility. Our current over-flow of staff and projected staffing needs would occupy most of that planned second Taylor facility.

Steve Wolens, a state legislator from District 103 in Dallas County, was the keynote speaker for the building dedication. He had cosponsored the legislation that created ERCOT. In his speech, he complimented all involved in the construction of the

Texas Electricity Market Evolution

<u>OLD</u>

<u>Supply:</u>	<u>Demand:</u>
Regulated by Texas Public Utility Commission:	
Vertically Integrated Utilities	Consumers
Independent Generators	(Residential, Commercial, Industrial)
Energy Marketers	
Governed by Public Power Contracts:	
Public Power Utilities	Public Power Consumers
(Municipalities & Cooperatives)	(Residential, Commercial, Industrial)

<u>NEW Texas WHOLESALE MARKET</u>

"Incumbent" means part of previous vertically integrated utility

<u>Supply:</u>	<u>Demand:</u>
Unregulated Competitive Market:	
Incumbent Generators	Retail Electric Providers
Independent Generators	(Incumbent and Newly Formed)
Energy Marketers	
Public Power Generators	Public Power Utilities
(Municipalities & Cooperatives)	(Municipalities & Cooperatives)

<u>NEW Texas RETAIL MARKET</u>

<u>Supply:</u>	<u>Demand:</u>
Unregulated Competitive Market:	
Retail Electric Providers	Consumers
(Incumbent and Newly Formed)	(Residential, Commercial, Industrial)
Governed by Public Power Contracts:	
Public Power Utilities	Public Power Consumers
(Municipalities & Cooperatives)	(Residential, Commercial, Industrial)

<u>NEW Texas Grid Reliability and Market Enablers</u>

Regulated by Texas Public Utility Commission:
Incumbent Transmission & Distribution Facilities
Newly Formed - The Electric Reliability Council of Texas ("ERCOT")

new building. He added that deregulation legislation provided the new foundation for competition. We needed a strong ERCOT to make it work. We were making progress, but there was a lot more to be done.

It was pretty well-known that the Dallas city government never wanted deregulation or the formation of ERCOT. That put a lot of pressure on Steve Wolens. He shared that pressure with us in the second part of his keynote address. As I recall, he said: "We are excited about this new facility. It will provide us with the best technology and ensure protection from any threatening weather conditions. Best of all, we now have two facilities to accomplish 100 percent redundant operations."

He then reminded everyone that legislators were not happy with ERCOT's performance. "Our deregulated 'retail market' isn't working," he said. "We need the 'retail market' to enable competition as we anticipated." He then delivered his punchline: "It needs to be fixed sooner rather than later. We want retail competition but will continue to fund that activity only if we know it can be fixed to work properly."

Politicians were really good at that. A pat on the back for a job well done, which included a final push toward the edge of the steep cliff already greased for you if you failed. I knew that there were problems but had been told they were just some technology issues that were already being addressed. I soon found out that they were much more than technical glitches.

Tom Noel, our chief executive officer, was on the hot seat. Steve Wolens's threat to the retail market, to shut it down if problems weren't fixed, wasn't news for Tom. He had already been raked over the coals about this at an earlier legislative meeting.

He was told, "We created you, and we can shut you down!" Tom's high-tech consultant, Monte Jones, smoothed it over with him: "Just technology issues, Tom. We'll find a new chief information officer to wrestle it down for you." Tom wasn't so sure about that. There had to be a business component to the problem.

Tom was in his late fifties—thin and about six feet tall, he was married with three grown daughters. Tom lived in Houston but had an apartment not far from ERCOT's Austin headquarters. He enjoyed all that Austin offered in culture, history, food, and entertainment. After the Wolens speech, it occurred to me that Tom might be living in an apartment instead of moving to Austin because legislators kept threatening to fire him.

But Tom didn't seem intimidated by Congressman Wolens or any other legislators. He had managed his way through political firestorms many times in his career. It wasn't his first time on the hot seat. He almost appeared to enjoy the challenge. He was concerned about our retail market operations problems but told those who might listen that he was confident ERCOT would get them fixed. He had a calm focus that said, *I've got this.*

Our chief operating officer, Sam Jones (no relation to Monte), was our grid operations guy. Sam was older than Tom and looked it too. He had a head full of gray hair and wore wire-rimmed glasses. A University of Texas engineer who was professorial in appearance, Sam was all Texas country boy through and through.

Sam was well known in the electric utility industry. Quiet, unassuming, and clearly in charge, Sam was the pick as COO at ERCOT's inception. He was an expert in electric grid reliability as well as a leader and iconic representative within NERC (the North American Electric Reliability Corp.) That's the premier electric utility industry standards setter and oversight group for the United States and Canada. Anything NERC roused Sam's attention.

The integrity of the Texas electric grid was Sam's focus. He knew the Texas grid like the back of his hand. He held a firm grip on our core mission of "We keep the lights on!" It was like part of his name. Of course, if the lights went out, we would first explain that we really didn't keep the lights on. We didn't own or operate generation or transmission and distribution facilities. That was the responsibility of those asset owners. I always had a hard time with the whole "we keep the lights on" core mission thing, but it wasn't my place to question an industry accepted sound bite.

Sam never said too much. He managed inside operations, while Tom handled the legislative and regulatory politics outside our operations. Sam had little concern for the retail market problems highlighted by Congressman Wolens. Retail market operations didn't impact grid reliability, meaning Sam had no responsibility for it. He was happy to leave retail market problems to Tom and Monte to solve.

ERCOT was also dealing with what appeared to be an imminent prospect of a project much larger than the one that would fix the retail market problems. There was talk of overhauling our entire ERCOT wholesale market operation. That would impact Sam, but he had no interest in the contemplated overhaul. From his vantage point, it had been a monumental task to get where we were with his grid reliability operation. Things were working well right now in the ERCOT wholesale market. Anything new would be a legislative, public utility commission, and stakeholder process issue and not an ERCOT management issue. His position was to steer clear of those processes until they came up with instructions for something new for him to do.

Sam's approach seemed too constrained. He was the expert on everything ERCOT wholesale market. Why wouldn't he be out front on the issue? If change wasn't needed, why not tell everybody? It wouldn't be long before I would learn why Sam kept his mouth shut—and I would learn the hard way.

Monte Jones had been engaged to advise Tom on what we needed to do both to fix the retail market problems and to get prepared for a possible major ERCOT wholesale market overhaul. His view was that ERCOT's main business was to provide a technology-based infrastructure and not a business-based one. ERCOT was simply about huge databases, 24/7 computer operations, and intricate communication channels. Monte assured Tom and Sam that all we needed was a chief information officer. And he pointed out that it was a safe bet, that with the growth of the internet and "the dot-com hangover," technology solutions would be the new driver of businesses. His rationale sounded right to almost everybody.

Tom wasn't so sure. Unlike Sam, he believed that any contemplated changes to our wholesale market operation would need quite a bit of *both* technology *and* business input from ERCOT. He felt even more strongly that business input from ERCOT was needed to complement any technology fixes for the current retail market problems.

Tom had clarified his thinking shortly after he had been given Congressman Wolens's ultimatum more than a month earlier at that legislative hearing about ERCOT's retail market problems. He wanted an energy markets, business-savvy lieutenant to oversee retail market operations, much like Sam did with "keeping the lights on" in our wholesale market. That lieutenant would also contribute to the brainstorming and debate for the ERCOT wholesale market overhaul.

Tom decided to hedge his bet. He had been told by Monte and some stakeholder representatives that he only needed a technology expert. On the other hand, Tom's business experience was telling him he needed another Sam-like business expert. He persuaded the board of directors that he should hire both Ken Shoquist as our new chief information officer and me as chief of market operations.

Fortunately for me, Sam went along with bringing me on board because I came with a recommendation from a member of the board of directors at NERC. Otherwise, my ERCOT odyssey never would have started.

4

The Initiation

I met Ken Shoquist for the first time at the dedication of the new building in Taylor. He was fair-skinned, with thinning reddish-brown hair and kind of a Jerry Mahoney puppet-like look. His thick, wire-rimmed glasses blurred his gray eyes. He appeared to be in his early fifties, about five foot ten, and he looked in pretty good shape. He was a little sweaty from the hot sun beating down on all of us. I guessed he had already been working the crowd for at least an hour before I arrived.

We shook hands. "Hi, Ray, I'm Ken. Good to meet you," he said. "We have a lot of work ahead of us, don't we?"

"We sure do," I said. "Good to meet you too."

Our first discussion grabbed my attention. Ken wasn't offensive, just a little strange. It felt more like he was spilling his guts to a psychiatrist than having a friendly chat. Ken told me about his being married and how his wife couldn't be there that day. Then it got strange when he proceeded to tell me that she had been detained in a Dallas jail because of some "phony charges" related to real estate fraud and how a paperwork error had blown things out of proportion.

Really? I wondered if he had shared that with Tom. No way that was true. Why hadn't it come up in his background check? That stayed in the back of my mind the whole time Ken was at ERCOT. I always suspected that Ken had told me that to assess my reaction as part of his sizing me up. I didn't like being more uncomfortable than I already was.

"Sorry to hear that," I said. "I look forward to meeting her. Sounds like she's a real go-getter."

"She sure is," Ken said. "Let's catch up tomorrow after our management committee meeting."

"Will do," I said. "See you then."

The conversation had been a lot different than any of the initial greetings I had had before with countless people I had met in similar situations.

Still, though, Ken was smart and smooth. To say he was politically savvy would be an understatement. He had already hit the ground running as he worked the crowd like a U.S. Senate candidate. He gushed with an air of competence and integrity. He passionately conveyed his technology prowess and technology vision for ERCOT.

All in attendance appeared excited about his arrival. They assumed that ERCOT had already confirmed that his technical training and experience were top drawer. He bolstered that assumption with his strong political skills, particularly in one-on-one interactions. I was impressed that he appeared to have developed a plan before he even arrived.

I normally didn't trust chief information officers. Not that they were bad people, but the title and officer level status never made any sense to me. What is a chief information officer, anyway? Nobody is responsible for *all* information. In fact, information technology people had no responsibility for the content or accuracy of any business information that flowed through the hardware and software systems they were assigned to maintain. Information technology is a support activity, not a leadership activity. It is mission critical in almost any business plan. But it was, in my opinion, never meant to be a lead dog.

From day one, I never warmed up to Ken. Some things about him bothered me, like that initial conversation, which had rattled me. In addition, I believed his resume was pretty weak for such a high-profile position at ERCOT. Nothing in it appeared to warrant consideration for an officer position. His resume showed no major hardware or application software project accomplishments. His experience was all unimpressive information technology maintenance and support activities with some minor participation in a few projects. I guess his last job, here in Austin at Dell Technologies, had made him a quick-fix candidate in the eyes of our high-tech consultant.

It was the politics that really made me nervous. Politics was always my biggest weakness. There was no question that God dealt me a bum card in that suit. Ken was dealt a perfect hand of political high cards. His ability to warm up to people and connect immediately with their basic needs was a standout initial difference between us. I took a step back and a deep breath.

I did what came naturally—I reminded myself that it was ultimately performance, not politics, that measured professional
competence.

It might ultimately come down to performance if you can survive long enough, but, today it was all about politics. Painting
a picture of ERCOT's future was a frequent request from those
in attendance. Ken was quick to assure everyone he met that he
already had a plan. He was here to make ERCOT's information
technology operation noteworthy for Sunday morning newspaper headlines. He said that it wasn't just hot air. It was a promise
that he would fulfill.

He also made use of that "brutally honest" tool. I overheard
Ken say to a Public Utility Commission staffer, "I have no idea what
Ray's job is here at ERCOT. Tom might be a bit confused about
his situation. I'm sure Tom and I will be talking about that soon."
Great. My new best friend was already painting a sad picture of
me before we'd even reported for our first day of work.

It was no secret that both Ken and I were high on Tom's succession planning list. Most outsiders and insiders believed it
to be a reasonable competition, but it did come with consequences. For me, it made relationships with legislators, public
utility commissioners, Public Utility Commission staffers, stakeholders, and all ERCOT employees far more complicated than
they should have been.

Welcome to the jungle, Dr. Livingston.

5

Why Are You Here?

Baking under that hot Texas sun and in the middle of the court-yard at the building dedication, I felt important but uncomfort-able. There had not been a general consensus as to my specific responsibilities. Even Tom couldn't provide a simple description of what he wanted me to do. He only pointed to my background to support his assertion that I was a great hire.

I was generally accepted as having the best business mind for whatever Tom wanted me to do. He had published a short bio introducing me, citing my extensive experience and qualifications as an industry leader. Everything in my resume validated my repu-tation for having top-notch business acumen.

For starters, I had an undergraduate industrial engineer-ing degree from Georgia Tech, as well as an MBA I had earned at Stanford. I was a certified public accountant, having achieved that certification while working at the world's largest accounting firm. I then served as a chief financial officer for an application software company that provided application software and consulting services to electric and natural gas utilities. I had been an innovator in the deregulation of the natural gas utility business since 1983. My most recent experience was with an incubator for-profit, ERCOT-like startup entity in the Carolinas. ERCOT was a logical next step for me.

In the late 1990s, I was an executive vice president with a New York City-based dot-com. Like most dot-com companies of the late 1990s, we had to bob and weave our way through cash short-falls to obtain lifeline funding from what I called "vulture capitalists." Back then, there were far more banged-up "dot-bomb" entities than shiny, successful dot-com entities. We got knocked around quite a bit chasing technology instead of a sound business plan. The lesson learned was to follow your business gut and don't chase all those shiny but ill-defined technology temptations. Take a look. You would see that knowing what business they were in, and not their leading-edge technology, was the key for any successful dot-com company.

Nevertheless, the technology boom was still in full bloom when I joined ERCOT in late 2002. If you didn't claim to be a technology-first entity, you were perceived to be out of touch. I didn't know it, but a lot of what I was to do at ERCOT would be to rescue people from the pitfalls of technology envy.

For Tom, it seemed like I was the complete package—engineering, business, accounting, application software, electric utilities, gas utilities, and deregulation. Like I said before, I also had the support of a member of NERC's board of directors.

As a consummate businessperson, I was always criticizing the fuzziness of the duties of a chief information officer. Of course, nobody at the building dedication cared about that. What they wanted to know was, "What do you do, Ray? What exactly is a chief of market operations?"

I was vulnerable to anyone who might decide to ask me that question. I was to take charge of a staff of about sixty people. I really had no idea what they did day-to-day. The good news was that they appeared to be a talented bunch. They worked hard but were swimming upstream, trying to hold the retail market together. It was impossible for me to construct a vision for my work at ERCOT from that.

I was called upon to paint a picture of that much sooner than I had hoped. It came when I spotted Tom talking to the Public Utility Commission staffer I had seen earlier conversing with Ken. After an enthusiastic "Welcome aboard," Tom introduced me to the staffer, Brad Estes, then excused himself to go talk to Congressman Wolens.

Brad and I exchanged pleasantries and talked a little bit about our backgrounds. He had graduated from Texas A&M with a degree in engineering. After ten years with the now-defunct Houston Lighting and Power Company, he had been hired by the Public Utility Commission, where he had now worked for five years. He was currently assigned to the team assessing the proposed overhaul of the ERCOT wholesale market.

He used that as a segue to talk ERCOT specifics. It was obvious to him where Ken fit in. He said, "Ken is going to fix the information technology glitches in the retail market and will lead ERCOT efforts to create the right technology environment to establish an ERCOT platform for any ERCOT wholesale market overhaul." He shared with me the generally accepted mission of ERCOT, "Most of my peers are pleased that ERCOT is finally realizing what business they are in. They believe that ERCOT is first and foremost a technology vehicle to facilitate deregulation." Then he popped the question, "So, Ray, what is a chief of market operations anyway?"

I didn't yet have an elevator pitch for that. I couldn't even explain it to him in five minutes. My thoughts quickly ran through the facts as I knew them. ERCOT is first and foremost charged with Sam's responsibilities to ensure the newly deregulated Texas electric grid doesn't fail. Our stated mission was "keeping the lights on" for Texas consumers, as stated in our annual report. Unfortunately, my people were not deemed critical to that mission. In addition, we weren't a technology group. So, why the hell did they need me?

I thought about the warning issued by Congressman Wolens and Tom's precarious position. It appeared to be the hottest topic in the room even without anyone mentioning it. That was it. I responded to Brad the best I could. "Tom and I believe that our problems are much more than simple technology glitches. Like Congressman Wolens said, the retail market problem is a pile of shit with a pony in it somewhere. With all due respect to my colleagues and technology experts, Monte Jones and Ken Shoquist, Tom thinks I'm the best-equipped person to find it, clean it up, and make it the envy of the world."

It wasn't an elegant response, but it addressed the big picture and gave the impression that I was a no-nonsense guy. Brad Estes didn't know exactly what I meant, but he was amused and satisfied to leave it at that.

6

Quasi-Governmental

We moved from the hot, sunny courtyard into the main conference room for the meeting of our board of directors, who numbered about twenty or so. Most of them were from the ten designated stakeholder groups of ERCOT. The board of directors would soon be reduced to sixteen members, four of whom were unaffiliated members not representing any specific stakeholder group. Sixteen still seemed to me to be an unmanageable number. How could anything get done? Unfortunately, that turned out to be only one of the many quasi-government political challenges central to my new job.

A young lady approached me. She was one of my officer peers. "Remember me? I'm Margaret Pemberton, our in-house legal counsel. Good to see you again."

We had met during my interview process. Margaret was easy to remember. She was taller than me and drop-dead gorgeous. Nicole Kidman immediately came to mind: sandy-blond hair, beautiful complexion, perfect figure. She was smartly dressed, fashionable and businesslike, and in her early thirties, I guessed. It looked like she had enjoyed talking her way through the courtyard of business executives and politicians, full of life and enjoying her high-profile role at ERCOT.

Margaret's approach to me was friendly but calculated. She understood that I was hired in part as a possible successor to Tom. She was open to giving me the benefit of any of her doubts but appeared to me to be unsure as to how we would interact. There was also that nagging confusion about my job description. I would be managing a staff that never interacted much with her. She offered no touchstone revealing a feel for where I fit in. I made sure our discussion didn't go there.

Margaret was a proud mother of a 4-year-old girl. Her experience included having worked for a large trucking company. She was no newcomer to having to deal with tough employees or even tougher customers. No doubt she could kick ass and take names with the best of them. She was well aware of her good looks and made sure they never got in the way of her credibility as our legal, regulatory, and stakeholder governance expert.

Her manner was direct, brash, and oozing with competence and confidence—almost too cocky at times. Her public utility experience fit perfectly with that part of her ERCOT responsibilities. All ERCOT legal matters, including all dealings with legislators, the Public Utility Commission, and stakeholder governance, had to go through her. I would later learn that her misguided, in my view, interpretation of the principles of ERCOT's quasi-government environment would adversely impact her attention to some purely legal matters such as vendor contracts.

Margaret had a genuine passion about ERCOT's cutting-edge activities. This was, after all, a big step up for her from being buried in the mundane assignments that dominate the work of typical corporate lawyers. This being a new level of work for her wasn't necessarily a good thing for ERCOT. I thought Margaret was missing some important experience by not having worked for a large corporate law firm. She lacked the experience of having to grind through the details of vendor and customer contracts, looking out for the fiduciary responsibility protection of clients. Unfortunately, the conventional wisdom here was that ERCOT didn't need that fiduciary responsibility focus. We were not an investor-owned stockholder corporation. We were quasi-governmental.

I really liked Margaret. I thought her experience at a trucking company would bring some healthy corporate cynicism with it, but it didn't. She drank only government "trust the process" Kool-Aid. Margaret was the first to earn a spot on my "good person with a bad business compass" list.

Margaret was a self-proclaimed quasi-government expert and was quick to give me a tutorial on that very subject. She was all in on the prescribed ERCOT stakeholder governance processes. She believed that the only fiduciary responsibility ERCOT officers had was to abide by those processes—to trust in them and for everyone to stay in their own lanes, so to speak. What I can recall her also saying to me was that she felt almost religiously obligated to stay in her legal-only review box, that stakeholders would tell us what to do and how to do it, period. Anything else would be contrary to our governance process, adding, in so many words, that it was not our place to intervene to enhance, accelerate, or impede stakeholder activities.

Margaret lost me at the "stay in your lane" reference. It made no sense to me. ERCOT contracts had to go through Margaret for approval, but she believed it was not her job to pass judgment on the need for the contract, integrity of any subcontractors, or the good faith negotiation of contract business terms and conditions. Statements of work, financial terms, and accountability for delivery were not her responsibility. She disavowed any hint of a fiduciary responsibility.

I had to give this a quick review in my mind's eye. Based on my interpretation of what she was telling me, there would be no cynicism on her part toward the judgment of ERCOT officers trusted with the approval of huge capital requests. No skepticism as to whether a contract approved by her made business sense. No examination of good faith business negotiations. No accountability. Her only job was to make sure contracts were legally enforceable. She seemed oblivious to the risk those blinders presented to her job security. Doesn't every officer have a fiduciary responsibility that is inextricably intertwined with the fiduciary responsibility of all the other officers?

Margaret was 100 percent comfortable with a blind trust in the representation of an ERCOT officer requesting the contract. It was that officer's responsibility to ensure that it was within the boundaries of stakeholder protocols. She trusted the representation by the officer requesting the contract that it was priced reasonably and negotiated appropriately. The hardest thing for me to accept was the fact that Margaret didn't believe she had a responsibility to ensure that the contract was for a valid business purpose. Also, she apparently believed she had no skin in the game related to the integrity of subcontractors or the ERCOT execution of the contract.

It struck a nerve for me.

I asked her, "What about officer fiduciary responsibility?"

She said, "We have none—we are a *quasi-governmental* organization."

Margaret proceeded to explain the logic behind how our officer responsibilities were different than those of "for-profit" corporate officers.

"It's really pretty simple," I recall her saying. "We have no investors in ERCOT ownership. No shareholders—we have no fiduciary responsibility. The concept of corporate officer fiduciary responsibility is a moot issue."

Whoa! What was that? No fiduciary responsibility?

I said, "Margaret—that is impossible. Officers always have a fiduciary responsibility."

"Not here," she said, adding that we were quasi-governmental—formed by the legislature, able only to do what the legislators, the Public Utility Commission, and the stakeholders told us to do. What I was hearing from her is that, from a financial standpoint, our hands were tied; the public utility commissioners approved our annual operating and capital budgets, which translates to an approved surcharge to electricity consumers. It is like a tax but is called a surcharge that is added to consumer electricity bills. We were simply doing what the stakeholder protocols tell us to do and doing it within the limits established by the public utility commissioners.

It still wasn't quite clear to me. I asked, " Then this quasi-governmental framework is far more governmental than 'quasi'?"

"Perhaps," she said, as best as I can recall, "but we are separate from the legislature—they have no legal responsibility for our actions."

Margaret's logic didn't end there for me. There had to be a catch.

"I guess we have no corporate legal protection like a private corporation," I said to her. "Doesn't that leave each of us even more exposed to individual fiduciary responsibility?"

Margaret took another sip of government process Kool-Aid, responding, "Of course not," while insisting our only exposure would be in not doing what we are told, in which case our only risk would be in getting fired. "It's really not all that complicated," she added.

There was no need to pursue this any further with Margaret. I thanked her for the tutorial and assured her I probably would have more questions later to fine-tune my thinking. Like I said, she was on my "good person" list, but I believed her misguided confidence on the issue of fiduciary responsibility would hurt her in the long run. I had no chance of convincing her of that right then.

Perhaps a review of the beliefs of James Madison, Alexander Hamilton, and numerous constitutional legal scholars concerning the fiduciary responsibility of government officials would change her mind. Things like the duty of care, the duty of loyalty, the duty of impartiality, the duty of accountability, and the duty of preserving the public trust in government had to be in play somewhere within ERCOT.

I was a businessperson, not a lawyer, and certainly not a legal scholar. Such a discussion with Margaret would have to wait for cocktail hour.

It was obvious that a simple tweak to my career mindset on fiduciary responsibility wasn't going to help me much. It was a sure bet that everyone involved with ERCOT tailored their behavior to be in sync with the makings of a quasi-governmental organization, as described by Margaret. Fiduciary responsibility should always be an officer concern, regardless of the organization's structure. Besides, even if it was only about getting fired, it wouldn't really be that simple. For one thing, there would be a big brand on your ass telling the world that you might not be trustworthy. Try getting another job after that.

The maze of processes that challenged anyone who participated in our quasi-governmental organization was a real brain teaser. It kept rattling around in my head. I tried to lock it away in a cerebral compartment, but I couldn't turn the key. There was something about puzzles that kept me from putting them down until they were solved.

I reviewed what I knew about the process. Stakeholders lobby legislators. Legislators pass legislation, then tell the Public Utility Commission what they want the quasi-governmental organization to do. Stakeholders tell commissioners how the quasi-governmental organization should do it. The Public Utility Commission issues a rule to the quasi-governmental organization as to "what should be done" and "how it should be done."

That rule has to be transformed into the quasi-governmental organization's operating procedures. The management of the quasi-governmental organization transmits the order from the

Public Utility Commission to its stakeholder process to derive operation protocols to comply with the rule. Stakeholders create the protocols through a process culminating with an approval of the ERCOT board of directors, which, coincidentally, is controlled by the stakeholders. The ERCOT employees then, and only then, implement those protocols with guidance from stakeholders to stay within their intent for the protocols.

Simple, right? It's so damn easy—we just do what we are told.

Our people at ERCOT might as well be programmed androids like the android props that entertained vacationers in the movie *Westworld*. The legislature controls the ERCOT theme park. The Public Utility Commission regulates its operation. The stakeholders control the ERCOT androids. No way an ERCOT android could go rogue, could it?

Then I thought about my initial encounter with Ken. Could he be like the Yul Brynner gunslinger? Could his brain have a program bug that would cause him to go rogue? That only happens in the movies, right?

It was making me dizzy. I was drunk on process overload. There would be plenty of time tomorrow to continue my adventure in all things quasi-governmental. I needed a break.

7

Sunshine on a Cloudy Day

After a full day of drinking from the quasi-government fire hose, I was happy to go home. Sue would be flying in from Atlanta in a few weeks. I couldn't wait for her to get there. Sue always had a smile for me. She always smiled—it was in her DNA.

We met in college. I first saw her on the opposite sideline at a fraternity intramural football game. It was crowded with players and spectators, but she stood out. She had blonde hair and blue eyes; she stood a little over five feet tall—petite, but not too skinny. She obviously took good care of herself. But it was more about ambience—she had a look that told me she was comfortable in her skin and enjoying this wonderful thing called life.

Sue was full of natural energy and enthusiasm. She couldn't help but be cute and beautiful at the same time. As we got to know each other, her inner sunshine and outward optimism continued to amaze me. I was really attracted to that, probably because I was so different. A classic case of magnetic bonding.

We were complete opposites. And we were instantly drawn to each other.

As for my being different from Sue, I always worried about something. To me, life was a burden, not something to enjoy. What the hell was I going to do the rest of my life? I always found comfort in worrying about big things like that when I no longer had any shorter-term worries, such as having to sift through the details of complicated lectures or prepare for exams that would either make or break my ability to pursue a desired career. I walked around under a dark cloud of cynicism and skepticism.

That wasn't all bad—regular doses of pessimism can help when taken properly. That dark cloud did keep me in close contact with reality. It kept me focused. Cutting to the chase to solve problems turned out to be one of my strengths. It served me pretty well, except when it made its way into a sarcastic remark.

But the dark cloud I carried above my head was doing what it does best. It kept out the sun, and I desperately needed sunshine. The dark cloud disappeared when I was with Sue. In fact, there wasn't even a dark cloud in sight. The thought of having her by my side the rest of my life was on my mind the moment I met her. Just like Smokey Robinson wrote it—*"I got sunshine on a cloudy day . . . my girl"* (songwriters: Ronald White and William "Smokey" Robinson Jr.).

It worked out as I had hoped. Twenty-eight years of staying on the same page and nurturing our three kids. We couldn't get enough family time, and we enjoyed the occasional trip by ourselves. We were a very tight family. Empty nesting was a big adjustment for us.

Surprisingly, the move to Austin took Sue's enthusiasm to a higher level. Her smile seemed brighter than ever. It drew me even closer to her. She always greeted me with a kiss and hardly ever asked me about work that day. No need to do that. I knew what happened, and Sue knew it most likely wasn't good. So we let it go.

"Hi, honey. Thought we should go out for some Tex-Mex for dinner. Maybe we could stop by the mall after that. I have some shopping to do." That's what I wanted to hear. I knew the drill—a little escape from the nagging politics and depressing uncertainties inherent in the grind at work. The shopping part was another part of her DNA. Early in our relationship, I thought it was her hobby—a fun, but costly, unintended consequence of her upbeat attitude.

Turns out it wasn't that at all. She enjoyed it all right, but she rarely bought things for herself. It was usually something for our kids, the kids in her class at school, our parents, a relative, a friend, pretty much anyone she knew that might need a reminder that they were special. My closet had a lot of things she bought for me. Some I never wore, but I kept them. They were great reminders to me of her always thinking of others.

From time to time, she would buy herself some clothes, but more than half the time, she would take them back. Might as well buy it on sale—you could always take it back. She loved that game.

I never had to make conversation. Sue had never heard of a pregnant pause. She told story after story. At times, her words drifted off into a stream of consciousness, losing track of a point she was trying to make. She thought that was so funny: "I forgot what I was trying to say. . . . Oh yes, well, anyway."

Sue's innocent approach to every conversation reminded me of Gracie Allen on the old *George Burns and Gracie Allen Show*. At times, her comments seemed scripted for a stand-up comic. I loved it. She would make comments that were difficult to discern. What was she really trying to say? When finally translated, it usually resulted in comedic relief. It wasn't a Yogi Berra-type thing. It mostly had to do with words with ambiguous meaning.

After years of experience, I became quite proficient in knowing what she was trying to say. One evening we pulled into a Dairy Queen for a couple of Blizzards. As we waited in the drive-through line, Sue was finishing up her stories about her day. We ordered at the drive-through speaker and waited for our turn at the pickup window. Sue loved anything sweet. She especially enjoyed milkshakes and Blizzards. She had a sweet smile of anticipation as the girl at the pickup window brought us our Blizzards. The girl turned them upside down then back to right side up as they were taught to do. Sue's smile had turned into a little frown. She looked at the girl and said "Oh, I'm sorry. We want them to go." The girl at the window had that look of "Seriously, lady?" Sue just sat there waiting for her to fix them to go. The girl didn't know what to do. I put her at ease. "Can you put lids on these Blizzards?" I asked. "We want to take them home to enjoy them." The girl realized what Sue was telling her. We got the lids and some chuckles as well.

Another time, I went to the hospital to get gallstones removed. Sue was with me in the holding area for the operating room. The intravenous bag was filling me with happy juice. It wasn't a risky surgery, but Sue was nervous, nonetheless. She never liked anesthetic situations. For her, any surgery seemed risky. When the time came for her to leave, I was pretty groggy. Sue said, "I'll see you on the other side. . . . " She paused, smiled, and giggled. "You know what I mean. Love you!"

I couldn't get enough of her sunshine. She was so alive and so enthusiastic no matter what the subject. Smart and creative, too. Upon her arrival in Austin, she quickly took the necessary steps to fill her days as a substitute elementary school teacher.

Sue was at the top of every teacher's list when they needed a sub. Their procedure was almost always the same. The teacher needing a substitute scribbled down the assignments for the next day. The sub was to follow those instructions but usually needed more detail than was in those instructions and had to make up things to do with kids that day. Substitute teachers always complained about that.

Sue not only expected that, she enjoyed it. The freedom to create on her own was much better than a detailed script. She had an uncanny ability to take fuzzy, open-ended assignments and make them meaningful for the kids. And those kids loved her. Sue turned what otherwise would have been a boring, meaningless day into a productive and fun day for the kids. I wasn't surprised that she was called to work almost every day.

Her favorite work was with first- and second-graders. Sue loved kids that age. It was fun for her to get totally in sync with their thinking. The kids loved her back. They even asked for her to be their substitute.

I'll never forget her story from her first day at a Texas elementary school. "It was a hoot today, honey," she said. "We started the day with the Pledge of Allegiance to the flag. When we finished, I sat down. But the kids remained standing. They looked at me like, *What are you doing?* I found out that after they pledge allegiance to the U.S. flag, they pledge allegiance to the Texas flag. I was so embarrassed!"

It was pretty funny, but it had an important hidden message. The Lone Star State. Texas pride. Texas-centric. It's all about Texas.

8

The Stakeholders' Golden Rule

It took a little time, but I did recover from the daylong information overload at the building dedication. I settled into my office at ERCOT. In keeping with my view of performance over politics, I made a location decision. Tom asked if I wanted a primary office at headquarters in Austin or at the new building in Taylor.

I chose Taylor to be close to my staff and close to the center of day-to-day operations. It would be good to be near my staff to get the needed face time with them to figure out what we should be doing to fix the retail market problem. I still had no job description, which was a significant issue because I was on the outside looking in at our stated core business of "keeping the lights on."

But there was a bigger picture. An office in Austin close to Tom would give me the time I needed with him to deal with the politics. I could also establish relationships with some of the key stakeholders who met there almost daily. Accumulating political capital would be an asset, but I knew I wasn't any good at it. Trying to exploit a weakness would probably blow up in my face, reaffirming Taylor as the right choice for me.

The importance of performance over politics drove my decision. I could control performance. I thought that I shouldn't have to worry about politics—*if I performed*. There was no question that a primary office in Taylor would make my political activities tougher right now. Politics did dominate the ERCOT landscape, but a primary office in Taylor with a primary focus on performance would be the best thing for me in the long run.

I needed to come up with a job description sooner rather than later. To ultimately determine my role, I had to gain more insight into what I needed to include in my survival kit. The only way to get those insights was to continue my exploration of the dangers and opportunities along the ERCOT quasi-governmental trail.

All stakeholders participated in what had been established by legislators as a quasi-governmental, all-inclusive process. ERCOT activities were guided by protocols determined through a stakeholder process, one created by stakeholders and that could be changed only by stakeholders.

Wait a minute. Stakeholders? Doesn't every man, woman, and child in Texas have a stake in ERCOT activities? They are all market participants, right? So how does this all-inclusive process actually work? I reached back into my mind's eye for that chart of Texas deregulation. It was all right there.

For our governance, ERCOT stakeholders were all the individuals and entities in the entire market chain, from electric generation through consumption. That chain began with electric generation companies and ended with consumer demand for electricity. There were millions of individual stakeholders and stakeholder entities in the chain.

Obviously, governance by millions of stakeholders wouldn't be practical for a quasi-governmental organization. Accordingly, each stakeholder was a member of an ERCOT stakeholder group. They communicated their opinions through those groups. They elected one stakeholder to represent their group. Those stakeholder representatives governed ERCOT through ten stakeholder groups. I kept another picture of this in my mind's eye:

ERCOT Ten Stakeholder Groups

NEW Texas WHOLESALE MARKET

"Incumbent" means part of previous vertically integrated utility.

Supply:	Demand:
Unregulated Competitive Market:	
(1) Incumbent Generators	**(6)** Retail Electric Providers
(2) Independent Generators	(Incumbent and Newly Formed)
(3) Energy Marketers	
Public Power Generators	Public Power Utilities
(**(4)** Municipalities & **(5)** Cooperatives)	(**(4)** Municipalities & **(5)** Cooperatives)

NEW Texas RETAIL MARKET

Supply:	Demand:
Unregulated Competitive Market:	
(6) Retail Electric Providers	Consumers
(Incumbent and Newly Formed)	(**(7)** Residential, **(8)** Commercial, **(9)** Industrial)
Governed by Public Power Contracts:	
Public Power Utilities	Public Power Consumers
(**(4)** Municipalities & **(5)** Cooperatives)	(**(7)** Residential, **(8)** Commercial, **(9)** Industrial)

NEW Texas Grid Reliability and Market Enablers

Regulated by Texas Public Utility Commission:
(10) Incumbent Transmission & Distribution Facilities
Newly Formed - The Electric Reliability Council of Texas ("*ERCOT*")

There was a stakeholder group for the former (1) incumbent large generation companies. There were groups for all other generation companies, called the (2) independent generators, and one for (3) wholesale power marketers. Those two groups were the most vocal and most paranoid about ERCOT involvement in stakeholder decisions. They always seemed tense. I guessed they were worried about someone or something getting in the way of their agenda.

There was one for (4) municipal utilities and one for (5) cooperative utilities—both were public power groups exempt from the Texas deregulation legislation, but they had to participate in ERCOT because they were inextricably interwoven into the wholesale market of the Texas electric grid.

There was a stakeholder group for (6) retail electric providers. Both incumbent and newly formed entities were in this group. Competition among the members of this group would be the focal point of problems associated with retail market competition.

The millions of household consumers were given their voice through a single (7) residential consumer stakeholder group. The other two consumer stakeholder groups were the (8) commercial consumers and (9) industrial consumers.

ERCOT worked most closely with the (10) incumbent transmission and distribution companies stakeholder group. We shared the common responsibility to enable grid reliability and market operations.

All the stakeholder groups elected their representatives to participate in ERCOT governance. They had a passion for innovation. They had a passion about the issues. They were good people. They all meant well.

The entire stakeholder process was founded with good intentions, but it had a fatal flaw. All the stakeholder representatives had a passion for strict adherence to what I coined The Stakeholders' Golden Rule. It was never documented, but it seemed a cultlike conviction of every participant in the stakeholder process. The Stakeholders' Golden Rule was easy to understand, making it easy to follow: "The ERCOT stakeholder process should never be impeded due to a rush for results or limit on spending. A rush for results or limits on spending would only yield less than an optimal result. *Texans would have only the best.*"

Most stakeholders would be quick to admit that the process wasn't perfect, but the totally inclusive, fair, open, and unencumbered nature of the process got pretty close to it. Besides, for the individual stakeholder representatives, it provided job security. It was a quasi-governmental nirvana governed by a utopian-like process. Representatives of the stakeholder groups plowed through endless meetings, seemingly unaffected by any hint of financial responsibility. The Stakeholders' Golden Rule allowed them to go about the governance of ERCOT like a smiling pack of *MAD* magazine Alfred E. Neuman disciples on steroids: "What, me worry?"

I understood the good intentions of the process, but the financially irresponsible adherence to The Stakeholders' Golden Rule ruined many of my days. It often came up in my daily activities and felt like a dentist hitting a nerve in my tooth when drilling out a cavity. In this environment, there was no fiduciary responsibility novocaine.

For capital spending on projects, that pain was brutal. No hard deadlines. No percent completion accountability. No incentives for on-time performance. Virtually unlimited capital funding. I never heard any reference to any limits. The band of Mexican renegades in the movie *Blazing Saddles* came to mind, with a slight modification: "Constraints? Constraints? We don't need no stinkin' constraints."

Clearly, the process was the only control over funding. There was no control over the process, which meant no control over the funding. Wasn't that ERCOT management's fiduciary responsibility? Quasi-governmental or not, the buck had to stop somewhere. Legislators and the Public Utility Commission staff weren't monitoring the details. They had no role in contracts or the progress of projects. ERCOT was the only entity with the people and detailed information to do those things. It seemed to me that every ERCOT officer had a fiduciary responsibility. Why wouldn't legislators, the Public Utility Commission, and stakeholders want to hold us to that responsibility? The answer was pure science fiction. Pure *Westworld*. We were only androids. Margaret was right. I was amazed at the comfort exhibited by ERCOT officers to buy into that code of conduct.

It was really hard to see how I could fit in. It wasn't a surprise that I never did. It was a daily struggle to try to cope with the discomfort I felt due to The Stakeholders' Golden Rule.

9

A Script for Everything

As the dog days of summer rolled by, I had to accept that I was flying solo on the whole fiduciary responsibility thing while continuing my quest for relevance. The review of the stakeholder processes didn't help me very much. It was quite a script. There was plenty of information to digest about ERCOT governance, but no bread crumbs there to help me solve my job description puzzle.

I turned my attention to revisiting what our annual report said about what business ERCOT was in. Somehow, the business I was to be in had to tie into or complement what was in our annual report.

The business of ERCOT was defined in our annual report as our mantra, "We keep the lights on." There were a lot of discussions about engineering issues and grid congestion issues, but, at the end of the day, it was pretty simple. Since electricity can't be stored, we were tasked to run a real time wholesale market to ensure the balance of electricity supply and demand throughout the Texas grid. With that, "We keep the lights on."

A short section at the end of the report addressed some retail market information. It didn't help me at all. It was hard to figure out what it was saying and why it was there. It clearly had nothing to do with "We keep the lights on."

I had to continue to look elsewhere to piece together my job description. I couldn't avoid it any longer. I had to take a deep dive into the activities of Sam's grid operation to at least understand everything about how "We keep the lights on."

In the Texas deregulation environment, electric generators would now compete based on electricity commodity pricing. That's right, *electricity commodity pricing*. The great debate about whether electricity should be an unregulated commodity or remain regulated as a public necessity raged on around the U.S. But here in the Lone Star state, there was no longer a debate. Electricity was to be a commodity. It was to be a commodity in a wholesale market between generation companies and retail electric providers.

It worked like this: Outside of ERCOT, generators competed by entering into bilateral contracts with retail electric providers. At any given time, about 95 percent of consumer demand could be met by those bilateral contracts. It was all conducted in an unregulated market outside of ERCOT protocols. Due to the uncertainty of the exact consumer demand at any point in time, roughly 5 percent of that demand could not be satisfied by those bilateral contracts. ERCOT had to implement a new market mechanism for buying and selling electricity to fulfill that approximate 5 percent demand to perfectly balance supply and demand to "keep the lights on."

The new market mechanism was for only about 5 percent of the total Texas wholesale market contracting. That small part of the entire Texas wholesale market became known as the ERCOT wholesale market. Much like the NASDAQ and New York Stock Exchange, the ERCOT wholesale market was the focal point for pricing electricity for the entire Texas wholesale market as follows:

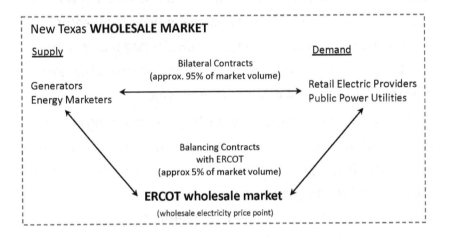

As you probably guessed by now, ERCOT ran that market exactly the way we were told to run it by stakeholders. The amount bought and sold had to be precise. ERCOT acted as agent for buyers and sellers to achieve that precision. We did that in real time 24/7. The combined NERC standards and ERCOT wholesale market protocols were the ERCOT script to "keep the lights on."

To get a complete understanding of the ERCOT wholesale market, I had to cover my fiduciary responsibility concern. I asked Sam about the core fiduciary concern in any market—creditworthiness. He said, "It's a non-issue. ENRON had assured everyone during the stakeholder formulation of the rules that ERCOT and stakeholders wouldn't have to worry about that." Too bad ENRON's credit problem had taken them down. They weren't around anymore to explain that to me.

I dug into it a bit more and found out that creditworthiness was an ERCOT issue but never a significant problem. Participants absorbed any small payment defaults. I knew that monitoring creditworthiness is typically a market operations function and could be included in my responsibilities, but it wasn't. It was managed through our ERCOT chief financial officer. That seemed reasonable to me, as long as someone at ERCOT had that responsibility. Of course, it was subject to stakeholder protocols. There would be no ERCOT judgment calls on a credit issue.

The ERCOT grid operation was a huge engineering challenge. We needed up-to-date information on all the physical characteristics of the Texas grid to simulate the entire grid operation 24/7. This included all the generating units and transmission and distribution facilities. We also needed the planned generation volume and extent of the commitments of generators to participate in the ERCOT wholesale market balancing services.

It required two NASA-like control centers in tornado-proof structures operating 24/7. They had to be located far enough away from each other to ensure redundancy under any circumstance. The control center operation was quite impressive. The 24/7 operation had to maintain real time precision—yes, literally, every second of every day. A large digital clock on the wall was a favorite highlight for visitors touring the center. Based on ERCOT's control of power flow, it showed how far the clocks at every home in Texas were out of sync with Greenwich Mean Time.

Generators, transmission and distribution facilities, and ERCOT operators followed processes and procedures established by NERC. Stakeholders were content with those standards and incorporated them into their protocols. Sam was responsible for ERCOT adherence to such details.

The NERC standards were created prior to deregulation for old, vertically integrated utilities to keep power supplied constantly and continually. Those standards evolved through decades of clarifications, refinements, and fine-tuning. NERC manuals spelled out processes and procedures in detail for almost any grid-reliability situation. To work in a control center, an employee had to be NERC-certified. Training and NERC certification was an ongoing NERC activity.

With deregulation of the Texas electric utility industry, ERCOT needed additional rules. NERC standards were still needed, but the new structure required even more standards. There were no longer vertically integrated utility entities responsible for balancing supply with demand. That balancing now took place in the new competitive markets; that is, the new bilateral market and the new ERCOT wholesale market.

The new ERCOT wholesale market worked well. From a process standpoint, as complex as it all really was, I can't remember even one NERC or ERCOT stakeholder protocol violation. Sam and his staff had it under control as scripted. It looked and sounded almost like rocket science.

But, as Margaret had told me, it's easy—just do what you are told. No matter how you examined it, she was right. There was a script for everything.

10

If You Don't Do
What You Are Told...

With a basic understanding of the ERCOT wholesale market operation, I looked for something that might warrant some input from my experience in energy markets. I knew the retail market problem should be my priority. It was still on everyone's list of simple technology fixes. Rather than dive into that right away, though, I thought a short look into the information gathering on a possible ERCOT wholesale market overhaul project could give me a short-term opportunity to show some relevance. Since it was only in an information-gathering stage, I thought I didn't have to be bound by just doing what I was told to do.

The Public Utility Commission had assumed responsibility for any rule to overhaul the ERCOT wholesale market. They conducted hearings to gather both old and new thoughts about an overhaul. Legislators let them have a free rein to pursue (or not pursue) any changes. It would be a project within the scope of the deregulation legislation already in place. There was no need for additional legislation. Let the stakeholders have at it.

The options ranged from doing nothing to a total rework. Revisiting the original discussions for an ERCOT wholesale market opened old wounds. The formerly agreed-to resolutions of old issues were resurrected for renewed negotiations. Everything was back on the table. It was a little different this time. Without ENRON in the mix, there was no political powerhouse to champion a new design. It did seem odd. The scars from the old battles were still pretty fresh. Consumers didn't want a change. So why change now?

There was political pressure from the federal government for ERCOT to conform its wholesale market design to that of the other ERCOT-like entities around the country. President George W. Bush was now in charge in Washington, D.C. He had appointed his former chairperson of the Texas Public Utility Commission, Pat Wood III, who had presided over the formation of ERCOT, as chairman of the Federal Energy Regulatory Commission. Wood's job was now to get all electric utilities around the country to buy into deregulation.

A number of larger electric utilities in the Southeast, Southwest, and Northwest weren't in the deregulation boat. They found ways to conform with federal deregulation guidelines in their own unique minimalist approaches with no deregulated wholesale market. The remainder of the electric utilities around the country were participants in ERCOT-like grids. They all had the same wholesale market design, except for ERCOT.

That was a huge problem for the Federal Energy Regulatory Commission. The minimalists argued that if Texas can do its own thing to comply with the new federal deregulation guidelines, why can't they? Wood, as chairman of the Federal Energy Regulatory Commission, was in a tough spot. As chairman of the Texas Public Utility Commission during the formation of ERCOT, he had been proud of that unique ERCOT wholesale market design. Now he wanted ERCOT to adopt a new wholesale market design to match the other ERCOT-like operations; his intent was to remove the minimalists' argument to conform in their own way.

Texans who wanted to keep the status quo and resist changing due to pressure from the federal government could easily justify their position. The physical infrastructure of the Texas grid allowed it to operate separately from the East and West national grids. Accordingly, the Texas grid was *not* under Federal Energy Regulatory Commission jurisdiction. Those who wanted to keep the status quo were outraged that Texans would even consider any change simply to fortify a federal political agenda.

The federal pressure worked its way into the thinking of the Texas Public Utility Commission. The three commissioners initiated a rulemaking proceeding, which, on its face, was exploratory. The "do nothing" option was still on the table. However, change was imminent to most observers, such as Tom.

The debates at the Texas Public Utility Commission were contentious. Each stakeholder group wanted revolution, evolution, or no change. The three commissioners were willing to listen. Stakeholders knew where they stood. The chairperson of the commission wanted change. One commissioner didn't want change. My read was that the third commissioner was not sure.

Every stakeholder believed that their own proposal was the logical choice. Each pitch in the debate was well prepared.

The landscape was different from the original collaborative effort. The first time around, the Lone Star State didn't have to consider the merits of activities in the other forty-nine states. This time, stakeholders would again bring in experts from outside Texas, but the views of the outside experts carried more weight. They would pontificate about the advantages of features of designs implemented by the ERCOT-like entities outside of Texas. Those arguments were typically logical and made a lot of sense. They also pissed off the stakeholders that didn't want any change. They were adamant about keeping the design as is. "We already heard all that," they would say. "No need to go backward and waste time debating it all again."

ERCOT management didn't have a dog in the fight. After all, we were to do only what stakeholders told us to do.

I believe Sam wanted to just keep the status quo, which didn't matter because he knew to keep his mouth shut.

For Ken, an ERCOT wholesale market overhaul would be the chance of a lifetime. It was the first explicit signal to me that his agenda had nothing to do with technology. It was all about money—lots and lots of money. He was all in on a revolution. With an ERCOT wholesale market overhaul, the table would be set exactly the way he had hoped.

Like me, Ken had been educated about The Stakeholders' Golden Rule. He believed that stakeholders would religiously abide by it—no rush, no spending limits, only the best for Texans. It was a perfect opportunity for some form of a skimming operation. His political prowess kept him from letting his excitement about a major change cause any conflict with stakeholders. He told them he would be ready to do whatever it was the stakeholders decided to do, even if it was to do nothing.

I made the mistake of poking my nose into the debate. I thought it was something Tom wanted me to do, but he never told me that directly. I shared my thoughts through testimony at the Public Utility Commission. It was an "out-of-the-box" suggestion to give consumers, through their retail electric provider, an opportunity to participate in a new day-ahead market to soften the blow of scarcity pricing in the real time market. Poking my nose into the debate turned out to be the biggest mistake of my twenty-eight years in business.

I earned a big fat blackball from the two most vocal stakeholder groups. Not surprisingly, they were the two groups with a vested interest in scarcity pricing—the independent generator stakeholder group and the energy marketer stakeholder group. It came with a shiny new suit of chains heavy enough to make Jacob Marley jealous. Throughout my remaining time at ERCOT, I had to carry around a painting of me with the title "the bad guy." It wouldn't be an understatement to say that my portrait was that of the Antichrist of the ERCOT wholesale market overhaul. They didn't know me, but they were relentless in their destructive commentary about me. Disingenuous, yet painfully effective.

Almost immediately after my testimony, I heard about it, not from Tom, but from the chairperson of the Texas Public Utility Commission. I had hoped for an initial first meeting with her to be on a more positive topic. Perhaps there would be some forward-looking content in our discussion to give me a chance to retain at least some credibility with her and her colleagues.

Rebecca Klein had been the chairperson of the commission for a little more than a year. Becky cared about ERCOT. Part of her duties as chairperson of the commission was to serve on ERCOT's board of directors. She was more than an administrative link between the commission and our board. She had a genuine interest in ERCOT's success.

She was a Texas native, a University of Texas alum, and a Stanford University graduate. I guessed that she had just turned forty, but looked like she was twenty-one. Dark hair. Petite. Pretty. She had big brown eyes that never allowed her to look angry. Becky was also a sergeant in the Air Force National Guard. I couldn't quite see her beating down new recruits or barking out marching orders, but she had a stout personality nonetheless.

Becky had a strong link with both Washington D.C., and Texas politics via a tour of duty at the White House under George H. W. Bush, which carried over to the current federal and state administrations. She had political aspirations beyond the appointment to the commission. Beneath her soft exterior was a layer of toughness. She could exchange punches with the best in politics.

After my infamous testimony, Becky invited me to breakfast. It was apparent from the start that she called me to help me, not to scold me. We had a common bond as Stanford graduates and as favorite targets of stakeholder complaints. It was obvious to her that I was a bit lost. "I know how you feel," she said. "It is a new challenge with no roadmap. We are all in this together. I have some suggestions for you."

Becky did read me the riot act about simply doing what I'm told and no more, but her delivery was soft and to the point. There was no mistake that I had screwed up and would not survive something like that again.

Her main message was not all negative. It was forward-looking as I had hoped. She encouraged me to stay away from the ERCOT wholesale market politics and focus on the retail market problems. She pointed out to me that the retail market effort would allow me more freedom because there was nothing to suggest anyone knew how to fix it. "Right now," she said, "the highest and best use of your experience has nothing to do with the 'ERCOT wholesale market.'"

I wasn't sure about the highest and best use thing, but it was clearly the only path available to extend my dubious but still useful employment.

11

To Switch or Not to Switch...
That Was the Question

My attempt to be relevant by poking my nose in the ERCOT wholesale market debate yielded a dry hole and a blackball. As Becky had said, it was time to stop leading with my wholesale energy market expertise and start solving the ERCOT retail market problem. Tom was intrigued with the prospect of an ERCOT wholesale market overhaul. But his job was on the line because the responsibility of the ERCOT operation to enable competition in the $30 billion Texas retail market was in the ditch.

I didn't fully understand all that was required for it to work properly. We knew the symptoms, but it was clear that nobody knew where we should begin to look for root cause problems. There was no "go to" model anywhere in the world.

It was easy to assume that the stakeholder protocols had been properly vetted and should work. It was also easy to place the blame on technology glitches. As the Public Utility Commission staffer, Brad Estes, and others believed, the root cause had to be a technology issue and the answer had to be a technology solution.

The good news was that my staff didn't buy into any of that. They knew the stakeholder processes inside and out. They had worked side by side with the ERCOT technology staff to put the systems in place. They had been monitoring system performance from day one. *There were no technology glitches.* No simple fixes. Everything, including the technology, worked as intended. The answer had to be a business issue, not a technology solution.

We first looked at the obvious symptoms. The most visible complaints were the growing dollar amounts of settlement and billing disputes to be resolved. The more disturbing complaints were from retail electric providers who claimed that they couldn't compete. Customers weren't taking advantage of their new choices of services and pricing options. They weren't switching from the incumbent retail provider to the newly formed retail providers.

Once again, I reached back into my mind's eye for that chart of Texas deregulation. Both complaints were symptoms embedded in business activity between consumers, the incumbent retail electric providers, and the newly formed retail electric providers. We knew that the problems were in the bowels of the stakeholder processes. It had to do with the timing and integrity of data gathering and data transfers, not software program calculation errors. We had business process glitches, not technology glitches.

Legislators adopted deregulation to achieve more than just wholesale competition. They also envisioned robust retail competition. Incumbent retail electric providers and newly formed retail electric providers would compete for retail customers. It got off to a pretty good start. More than one hundred newly formed retail electric providers were implementing marketing strategies, advertising campaigns, and new products packaged with incentives to entice customers to switch from their incumbent retail electric provider.

But switches weren't happening at an acceptable rate, and retail competition sputtered. By default, the problems with the switching process caused the incumbent retail electric providers to hold too big a competitive advantage.

That wasn't the intent, but it was what came out of the stakeholder process. Switch transactions were the consummation of a customer switch from one retail electric provider to a different retail electric provider. The relevant stakeholder protocols required switches to be consummated only upon completion of a requested meter reading.

A request for a meter reading was initiated with the notice of a switch. The switch was completed after the requested meter reading took place. It looked like a simple, harmless process. But it was a process that broke down with any data-entry error or error in the timing of the transfer of data among the retail electric providers, the transmission and distribution companies who owned the usage meters, and ERCOT. Those errors caused data integrity problems. And they were related solely to business processes. Compounding the problem was the issue of a new switch request during the period of a pending meter reading request. There were no stakeholder protocols for that. It was another business process problem for us to solve.

Errors piled up, and switching activity continued—only at a disappointing low rate. It was deemed easiest for a switch to take place at the next normal monthly meter reading instead of on a specially requested meter reading date. That meant that a consumer transaction to change retail electric provider had to wait until the next monthly meter reading cycle. During that wait, the incumbent retail electric provider had plenty of time to convince the consumer to stay with them. Consumers weren't switching. There was too much of an advantage for the incumbent retail electric providers.

The only solution that got legs was always referred to as a technology solution. It was the notion of an immediate transition to automated real-time usage meters at more than six million retail consumption properties. It was the ultimate solution to the data integrity problems, but it was not practical. The inability for ERCOT to make that immediate transition was the alleged "technology glitch." Obviously, Steve Wolens and his colleagues had been sold a bill of goods. It was not a simple technology glitch that ERCOT failed to fix. It was a failure of the stakeholder process to put protocols in place to enable a business process transition over a period of years to procure, test, and install the six million-plus automated real-time usage meters. The stakeholders were aware of the existing business process challenges. They had no answer for the switching problem, but they knew we had billing disputes. Under our current process, we could never achieve 100 percent accuracy. They didn't know if the errors resulting in disputes were all data-integrity errors, all calculation errors, or a combination of both. So, they agreed on a protocol to address that. A 2 percent overall retail market dollar error would be acceptable, subject to dispute resolution. That business-process fix was the stakeholder protocol for dispute resolution to be relied upon until the six million-plus automated real-time usage meters could be implemented.

Resolving disputes between retail electric providers took time and never stopped growing. The total disputes amount was approaching $1 billion. The large overall amount was a concern, but, more importantly, individual disputed amounts were too big a financial burden for the newly formed retail electric providers. The way I figured it, a 2 percent overall retail market dollar error could actually result in more than a 10 percent error for many newly formed retail electric providers. It was an unacceptable financial burden for those new companies.

There was also the collateral damage that sometimes made its way to Texas consumers. A switch that a consumer thought had occurred might not have happened. ERCOT had nothing to do with end-use electricity consumers, but we were tagged with that problem.

Questions and complaints about the switching process flooded our call center. They were not just from our stakeholders but also from end-use electricity consumers. Switching problems and billing disputes were piling up with no end in sight. Complaints from retail electric providers to legislators and the Public Utility Commission staff could not be ignored. Those complaints often recommended that the Public Utility Commission and legislators shut us down. Steve Wolens had relayed that message to us months before at the dedication of our new building in Taylor. We had to come up with a solution.

At least I finally knew why I was here. I surprised myself. My wisecrack comment to Brad Estes at the building dedication was spot on. I really did need to pull the pony out from under that pile of shit.

12

Got It

There it was. A real job for me at ERCOT. Worrying about what to do had made the summer heat hotter for me than for others. I could finally breathe easier, and Sue and I could now enjoy our first fall living in Austin.

The retail market was in the ditch all right. I was now all in with my staff to fix this thing. The two most visible complaints, the unacceptable sputtering of retail competitive activity and rapid growth of ERCOT wholesale market settlements and billing disputes, were symptoms, not the actual problems we needed to solve. It was time to get out of brainstorming mode. We had identified the patient's symptoms well enough to know where to search further for root causes.

In this case, the stakeholder process was *not* what we had to follow. That would only continue to make things worse. Stakeholder protocols had to change to enable the one-of-a-kind Texas deregulated retail market to flourish. We had to be sure that Tom, the board of directors, the Public Utility Commission staff, and all the stakeholder groups understood and accepted that fact. They had to. The alternative was failure. It would be a relief to get out of android mode for a while.

We were still a long way from a solution, but we had confirmed it was all about business processes to enable the phasing in of the ultimate desired solution to implement six million-plus automated real-time usage meters. I now had enough information to reorganize my staff in a way that would work in both the short run and long run. It would be a challenge. I would leverage my accounting expertise and business acumen. My energy-markets experience would stay on the sideline. At least I knew now that ERCOT was more than "keeping the *fucking* lights on." For the first time, I was excited and comfortable with my job at ERCOT.

I had my elevator pitch:

We are in the business of enabling robust retail competition, and we are in the business of timely and accurate market settlements. To be sure stakeholders are properly informed and that ERCOT remains in lockstep with stakeholder needs, we are also in the business of ensuring stakeholder satisfaction.

I delivered the message to the ERCOT board of directors at their monthly meeting. All who needed to know were either board members or attending as observers. It was the best way to get the word out to all the right people. I finally did something politically correct. The presentation was short and to the point. Well, not really short, but it was as clear as I could make it at that time:

"We all know that the retail market is in the ditch. We all also know that the Texas 'retail market' initiative is the first of its kind in the world—there is no blueprint for how it should work. We stumbled through its start because the initially adopted protocols don't address enough details in the business processes to achieve the intended Texas 'retail market' responsibilities.

"A technology fix to incorporate six million-plus automated real-time usage meters across the state is the answer in the long term, but we still don't know the extent of that project. It will likely require some kind of phase-in over five or more years. We can fix our problems now without them. In fact, we can modify our protocols and fine-tune some of the ERCOT mathematical techniques related to load profiling to both work in the short run and easily plug into the project still being planned to procure, test, and install automated real-time usage meters in the long run. We do not see a need for a major technology overhaul. We will work with Ken's staff to make any needed information technology modifications.

"We will work within the stakeholder governance process to seek approval for the modified ERCOT protocols. We have begun discussions with the transmission and distribution stakeholder group and the retail electric provider stakeholder group to identify the changes needed to both their business processes and ERCOT business processes. Those stakeholders know the ball is in their court to make this work. We are all excited about fixing this thing.

"My staff will take on the task to establish and maintain the infrastructure to: (1) fulfill ERCOT's objective to enable competition; (2) fulfill ERCOT's obligation for timely and accurate settlements; and (3) ensure stakeholder satisfaction. Going forward, that is the business my group is in."

Stakeholders seemed to be relieved for me to step aside from the ERCOT wholesale market overhaul debates. Even the blackballing stakeholders were pleased, although they seized the opportunity to characterize my approach in a negative context. They invoked an old cliché: "Even a blind squirrel stumbles upon some nuts from time to time."

There was no argument with what I wanted to do. Since the two stakeholder groups impacted by the change had already agreed with our proposed solution, the board of directors gave tacit approval to the plan. As long as I wasn't asking to significantly expand my staff or spend money on consultants, I could pursue solutions however I wanted.

Some board members still weren't sold. They weren't about to go on record to say that the answer to our retail market problem was business-based, not technology-based. It was still a lot easier to point to the installation of six million-plus real-time usage meters as the only fix to the problem. That had been our excuse to legislators all along.

An unaffiliated board member weighed in on that point, "So, Ray, how do you propose we inform Steve Wolens that he has to wait five years for us to get out of the ditch?" I reiterated that we had a one-year plan and that the transmission and distribution stakeholders and retail electric provider stakeholders were confident that this solution to the disputes and customer switching concerns would work for however long it might take to phase in all the automated real-time usage meters.

Some board members were impressed. They had been hoping for some hope. They, too, had heard Steve Wolens loud and clear, and they wanted at least to have a plan. Another unaffiliated board member chimed in: "Sounds good, Ray! Please keep us posted on your progress." It was my very first "attaboy" from anyone at ERCOT.

For my staff, the escalated interest in their work was just what the doctor ordered. The constant repetition of the ERCOT mission—"We keep the *fucking* lights on"—did nothing for their morale. Yes, I was already tired of hearing that phrase, but I knew I just needed to get comfortable with it somehow. My staff always knew that had nothing to do with their jobs. They welcomed the higher visibility of the importance of their work. They weren't afraid of the new challenge. Just the opposite. They were re-energized.

13

Pocket Aces

My staff was seasoned. All had quite a bit of experience prior to coming to ERCOT. Pretty much all of them had worked on the development and implementation of the current retail market process from its inception. About sixty-five people were now with us full time. I'd say that the average age was about thirty-five. About half had college degrees. We had no contractors or outsourced work. All in-house personnel for routine processing, putting out fires and small project work.

I knew my staff had already been through a lot and continued to face new challenges. They were the ERCOT front line in the trenches with stakeholders. They expected long hours and hard work every day. All they got for the long hours and hard work was criticism from legislators and constant complaints from stakeholders and consumers. It was no knock on their work ethic. Theirs were just thankless jobs.

It was natural for them to resist a new leader from the outside who had no clue what they did. It didn't help much that I managed to quickly earn a stakeholder blackball. Nothing like putting your confidence in a political wet noodle to drag you out of the mud.

My first task was to meet face-to-face with each potential manager-level staff member. It was important that they knew that I cared about their concerns. It was both an icebreaker and positive way to get the picture of the landscape that was in their mind's eye. I needed those pictures to give me ideas as to the best structure and placement of personnel in my reorganization. I also took that opportunity to share my thoughts on why I got off to a slow start. The hope was that my honesty would give them some comfort. It turned out to be a good idea. It did get us started on the right foot.

I was literally in awe of the talent, depth of experience, and positive attitude of every staff member I met. The essentials to succeed were there. As I look back, I realize that I didn't want to replace any of them. All were technically astute and passionate about ERCOT and our work. From the smallest details of the processes and procedures through the technical expertise required to integrate those processes and procedures with the inner workings of the computer hardware and software. They knew it all.

In addition, they possessed the ability to deal with uneven hour-to-hour workloads. They understood the reasons for that. It went with the excitement of being part of something new. The development of something that hadn't been done before was why they joined ERCOT. They were committed to making our invention work.

My staff deserved the boost they got from the exposure with the ERCOT board of directors. Now they needed to be organized for the best chance for success. The approach was to have the right people in the right roles, in which their natural tendencies drive their performance. It would be in keeping with the old adage, "You can lead a horse to water, but you can't manage it to drink." We needed director- and manager-level leadership. We didn't have the luxury of time to waste managing people.

Our organization had to fit with the business we were in. We needed a team of surgeons to find the underlying problems causing our patient's symptoms. They needed to properly identify the exact problems, fix them, and put in place an appropriate maintenance plan to keep our patient healthy. We also needed time—lots of time—to keep stakeholders happy while we performed the surgery and to provide appropriate post-surgery monitoring of our patient's health.

I needed two lieutenants: a master surgeon and master communicator. No time for training. In fact, the best scenario would be to have two lieutenants who were already qualified to function as officers at other organizations. I needed at least two years from them to get things done and to nurture their people. Political savvy was of paramount importance. As much as I would try, it was highly unlikely that my political efforts would be enough.

I inherited the most respected ERCOT employee other than Sam. It seemed like Jim Galvin was preordained to be my master surgeon. It was hard to believe I could get that lucky after all the bad luck I had since I started. I felt like the teenage kid in *Animal House* who had a Playboy bunny look-a-like pop into his bedroom through his window: "Thank you, God!"

Jim had searched for me among the packed crowd of Texas dignitaries at the dedication of the new building. When he found me, he was already in lieutenant mode. He took it upon himself to make me comfortable. I wondered what he was thinking. I must have looked totally lost when he first saw me. He sensed what was going on and thought he probably would feel the same way in my situation. Nothing unusual. He introduced me to some stakeholders. Jim took me under his wing and made it clear that he was happy to have an opportunity to work with me. It gave me a boost to get through that stressful day.

Jim was in his mid-forties, but looked older than his years. He had deep-set piercing blue eyes and a dark, ruddy complexion that looked like he had worked outdoors most of his career. His hair was more gray than black, and he combed it straight back like a Mafia boss. Average height, heavyset with Popeye forearms, he had a hardened appearance that made me think of a fine piece of sculpted ceramic that had been put through intense heat to give it strength and rigidity. Jim must have been through some heavy-duty character-building experiences.

I found out that was exactly the case. Jim was a former golf pro—what was known as a "grinder"—taking on the next challenge while not pouting about lost opportunities. A tournament golf pro has nowhere to hide. Any weaknesses are totally exposed to your fellow competitors, spectators, and tournament officials. Your score is all you have to show for your effort. It is the only way you are rated. Nobody cares about your perfect swing. Nobody cares about your ball-striking ability. Nobody wants to hear your excuses. One mistake and you miss the cut. How many people have worked a job where they got paid, not for participating, not for working hard, but only for superior performance? Jim didn't need a fancy resume to qualify for a leadership job. The necessary instincts had been burned into him during every competitive round of tournament golf.

We bonded pretty quickly. The golf thing was the perfect topic for discussion. It wasn't the traditional executive to executive golf chitchat. I liked to play golf but wasn't a fanatic fan of the PGA Tour. We talked about the pressure cooker of competition.

My son had spent a few years as a golf pro on the minitour circuits. Sometimes I caddied for him. Most of the time, I just watched. He worked so hard and didn't have much to show for it. Very little in earnings and some wrist and back problems from working so hard on the driving range. Most people don't appreciate the value of a golf pro experience. It's about the development of intangibles that yield a long-term payback in life beyond golf.

I was certain that Jim approached this job like he approached his golf game. Meticulous attention to every detail and an inherent need to perform perfectly every time. Jim knew what it was like to have the rest of his life tied directly to his next golf shot. Dealing with complex challenges, both technically and politically, was a piece of cake when compared to that. I wasn't surprised that Jim was clearly respected by all attending the building dedication. He had developed the skills that earned him that respect before he took his first job in the business world.

Prior to joining ERCOT, Jim worked for the California grid operator, a statewide quasi-governmental entity much like ours. He brought with him valuable grid operation experience. He knew the details of Sam's operation. He was an expert on ERCOT whole-sale market activities. He also had worked closely with the information technology operations. The knowledge of how it all worked together came with him from California.

Jim retained so much from his cumulative experiences that he could tell me almost exactly how everyone fit in the ERCOT structure. His job at ERCOT was primarily wholesale market settlements. That appeared to be working well. Our information technology people liked him. Jim knew enough about their operation to create the perfect business/technology interface for ERCOT wholesale market settlement activities.

Jim was also responsible for our retail market switch transaction activities. That wasn't working well. The Texas retail market was not just unique within the U.S. but also unique worldwide. There was no California experience or any other place to find help with that problem. Jim and I were well aware of the water in which we were swimming. With Jim's knowledge of the ERCOT operation and my business and accounting background, we made a pretty good leadership team to address the retail market challenge.

Our ability to work well together was supported by our shared view of business versus technology. Jim was frustrated with the current ERCOT bias in favor of the information technology group to head up all problem-solving activities. He worked his way through that to get the settlements process to work. But the pressure for the information technology group to be center stage on the retail market work only confused any attempt to make progress. From his standpoint, it was one of the reasons we were stuck in the mud. He was certain that our problems were rooted in people, processes, and procedures and not in computer software bugs or glitches. I told Jim, "Amen, brother! I agree! Let's get to work."

I also needed a politically savvy lieutenant to work full time communicating with stakeholders while Jim stayed focused full time on our technical work. It was an opportunity for me to get another lesson in ERCOT quasi-governmental processes.

Hiring people from outside to fill a new position was another quasi-governmental organization enigma. The new position had to be included in the approved budget. On top of that, the new job's job description had to be approved by human resources, then posted for a certain time period before a hire could be made. Responses to the posting were reviewed by the human resources department, which forwarded resumes of candidates they deemed acceptable to the businessperson owning the job opening. The business owner notified human resources as to the candidates to be brought in for interviews. Second interviews were often required before a final hiring decision could be made. If the business owner didn't get any resumes that fit what they wanted, they would submit a revised job description for human resources to approve and post again. Once a candidate was selected, human resources did a background check.

I had been through such processes before. In fact, I managed a similar process as a chief financial officer for a few years. The most important part of the process was the background check. ERCOT's human resources guy, Gary Stroud, was pretty reasonable. He recognized that the front-end job posting, resume accumulation, and resume culling part of the process sometimes had limited or no value for the hiring manager. He still made sure that he always did the background check. The worst thing would be to hire somebody with questionable character.

My new politically savvy lieutenant would be charged with the objective to maximize stakeholder satisfaction. He/she had to be an experienced and credible leader of stakeholder liaison activities. Traditional utility customer service technical skills were required. But we needed much more than that to effectively liaison with the ERCOT stakeholder gangs. In-depth knowledge of the business of every stakeholder in the Texas electricity delivery supply chain would be ideal. A current or ex-employee of a Texas stakeholder wouldn't fit. There would be too much perceived bias. And, if not living here, they would need to move their family immediately to a commutable distance from both our headquarters in Austin and our primary operations center thirty-five miles northeast in Taylor.

Gary said that those qualifications were unique enough to waive posting for the job. He asked if I had someone in mind. I told him that I did. We got Tom to sign off on it. I could get the person I knew would be the perfect fit.

Rich Gruber was an exceptional executive. He was a forty-two-year-old Dale Carnegie clone who could have written an even better book on how to win friends and influence people. We had previously worked together for more than ten years and were energy deregulation junkies from the eighties and nineties.

Rich started his career in Houston with a major natural gas pipeline company. Those years took him through the deregulation of natural gas pipeline companies to transform natural gas from a regulated scarce resource into an unregulated commodity.

When I reconnected with Rich, he was a vice president of customer service for a utility in the Northeast. He was excited to hear about the opportunity to return to deregulation mode. His wife was from the Dallas suburbs and a graduate of the University of Texas. She was eager to return to Texas, especially Austin. He accepted our offer and made the move to Austin.

Anything related to stakeholder satisfaction was Rich's responsibility. His people were knowledgeable enough to answer most of their questions, but, if they couldn't, they would connect them with the right ERCOT people. It included being proactive. They contacted each stakeholder group member at least once a month to see what was happening at their company. Rich was also charged with ERCOT support of the stakeholder committee meetings. We reserved meeting rooms and coordinated meeting notices. We attended those meetings and followed up with any ERCOT assignments. The retail market call center we had set up for the high volume of calls from retail electric providers and consumers was another part of our stakeholder satisfaction operation. Those calls were really tough to deal with, because many of them had to do with things outside ERCOT responsibilities.

Rich was at his best working a room of stakeholders or on the telephone with them. He was politically savvy. He could discuss any part of a stakeholder's business. It didn't take long for him to get to know every stakeholder representative. Even the blackballing stakeholders were comfortable with Rich. Yep, I needed him.

I might have been feeling a little too good about our chances to succeed. Jim focused on pulling retail market competition out of the ditch while maintaining accurate wholesale market settlements and billings. Rich was masterful at keeping stakeholders off Jim's back while he addressed the retail market fixes. They worked well together in always making sure that stakeholders were informed and in sync with our activities.

With Jim and Rich, I held two pocket aces. No way could I lose with those two guys.

DECEIT

14

Business vs. Technology:

Who Tells Whom What to Do?

Jim, Rich, and I were on the same page on the whole business vs. technology thing. Technology was implemented to support business, not vice versa.

All around the world, the scope of the job of information technology professionals had grown exponentially. Personal computers with powerful software tools, the internet, search engines, portals, wireless routers, smartphones, etc. Their information technology maintenance and support job evolved into a whole lot more than a reboot of a mainframe system. They were expected to know everything, chapter and verse, about past and current technologies as well as technologies contemplated for the future.

Businesspeople's understanding of how the new technologies worked had also grown exponentially. Technology was no longer a black box. Businesspeople readily understood data storage limits,

I/O constraints, processor speed, and how to optimize overall information technology productivity. Perhaps their biggest leap forward was the utilization of new software tools and software applications. Most of the time, businesspeople knew more than the information technology people did about how they worked and how they were used. They had to. Their business processes and procedures had to interface properly with them.

There was no longer a clear line between business staff and information technology staff. Both claimed the leading role for business changes, and both wanted improved productivity. Neither wanted to be branded a dinosaur. So, who tells whom what to do?

The information technology staff would warn decision makers that without the latest technology, the organization would lose its ability to compete. Businesspeople cited their urgent needs for immediate productivity improvement. They couldn't put things on hold waiting for the latest and greatest tools. Organizations had to decide between implementing processes and procedures using tried and true technology versus implementing processes and procedures for leading-edge technology that business people sometimes referred to as bleeding-edge technology. Using current technology was critical. Business processes and procedures were critical. Who was the lead dog?

From my perspective, the right answer was the task of putting in place business processes and procedures that could readily adapt to changing technology. For Jim, Rich, and me, it seemed obvious that it was a task for business, not technology, people. We all had proven track records of success with that approach. Business was always the lead dog.

For Ken and his staff, nothing could be further from the truth. Technology was a cornerstone operation for every part of our business. The latest technology could readily adapt to changes in business needs. Business requirements were just inputs. The right technology infrastructure was the most important consideration. Texans couldn't be left in the Dark Ages. Information technology was the lead dog.

For almost any discussion, the elephant in the room became the political struggle as to who was in charge—business experts or technology experts? It was a new common problem confronting every organization with a chief information officer. For the non-operations ERCOT officers, it was only an elephant in the room. For Sam and me, it was a little more important.

Sam's business of "keeping the lights on" was a business rich in its use of technology. The industry standard for "keeping the lights on" was to implement an entirely outsourced information technology project. ERCOT was no different. Upon completion of the project, the hardware and software were transferred to our operations facility for testing and approval. The maintenance and support of the platform were provided by the same outsourcing companies. Ken's responsibility was limited to working with the outsourcing companies to maintain and support the hardware and communications facilities in their platform. Sam was the primary interface with the outsourcing companies. He didn't need to interface much with Ken. There was no political struggle. Sam and his business experts were in charge.

I had hoped to have the support of Sam on the business vs. technology issue when addressing the retail market side, but I didn't. He hadn't bought into our business approach to fix the retail market. He didn't know enough, nor did he want to know enough, about how the business vs. technology leadership should be applied to the ERCOT retail market operation. From Sam's point of view, Ken seemed to know a lot more about his job than I did about mine. The wind was behind Ken. The politics were in favor of technology. That meant that Sam had no problem with technology being the retail market lead dog.

Ken sensed he had a big advantage in our political struggle. It was another partisan opportunity. I became the reluctant model for another demonizing picture, and Ken painted me as an anti-technology guy—a real dinosaur. I was an eighties executive retread out of touch with technology-savvy legislators, Public Utility Commission staff, and all of our stakeholders. He and his staff tactfully worked that picture into the thinking of my peers and the ERCOT stakeholders.

That bothered me even more than having to work around the stakeholder blackballers. My entire career was centered around implementing efficient and effective solutions to integrate business and technology. Blowing me off as just old news really pissed me off.

Tensions grew as it got harder and harder to work around the "Business vs. Technology" elephant in the room.

15

Not Enough Time to Do a Background Check

The technology experts remained at the forefront of all our stakeholder interactions, but Jim and Rich did a good job of communicating our business-process-first approach to the retail market issues. It kept stakeholders satisfied. Both business and technology were properly focused. The stakeholders couldn't ask for more than that.

Ken took the next big step in his plan, which I perceived was to set the cornerstone of the foundation for what in my estimation was a conspiracy. He obtained approval to hire a lieutenant to administer *all* ERCOT project funding. It was the right time for him to make the move. He held the cards. He made it look like the new position fit just right. The new lieutenant would oversee all project funding and project progress. Tom, Sam, and Margaret were all in with Ken. It was no surprise to them that it made no sense to me. Tom would approve the move.

Our chief financial officer, Maxine Buckles, wasn't so sure it made sense, either. It was also my opinion that she didn't like turning complete control of project administration over to Ken, and that would likely be because she knew that in the grand quasi-governmental scheme of things, sole control of that process meant sole control of the money. It appeared to me that Maxine was being removed from her financial oversight role related to capital spending. A control that ERCOT needed was being removed. I believe Maxine was in a position to raise the red flag, but she probably figured it was best to avoid the conflict because she knew the politics and the quasi-governmental script. The burden was on Ken to do an honest job, and it seemed she would mind her own business. She would keep her blinders on to ensure the proper recording and timely payment of project expenditures. Nothing more. Like Margaret, she would stay in her lane.

I was asked to interview Ken's job candidate, Steve Wallace. He reminded me of a large cherub. Heavy but not fat, with rounded features. Round shoulders. Round hands. A round belly and a distinctly oval-shaped head. Short black hair. Mid-forties. Never a frown on his face. A real charmer. His persona was that of the cat who just swallowed the canary. I shouldn't have made any assumptions. You never know what is behind an outward appearance, but I just couldn't get comfortable with him.

Steve was allegedly highly qualified. His most recent work had been as a partner in a worldwide accounting firm. That caught my attention. In my first job out of graduate school, I had earned my CPA while working for a Big 8 accounting firm. A distinct characteristic of alumni of CPA firms is their clear answers to questions. The way I saw it with Steve, he never gave a straight answer to my interview questions. No way, I thought, this guy had ever been a partner for a large accounting firm. That had to be a misrepresentation, I reasoned. Strike one against Steve.

Ken introduced Steve as both a technology and business expert. He would be well-suited to fill the gap in ERCOT's ability to integrate business with technology. From what I gathered in talking with Steve, Steve was strictly a key fob-carrying, Excel and PowerPoint guy—that he had never developed any large database software applications of any consequence for any entity, which, to me, meant he had no business experience with anything remotely related to our retail market project. From what I could tell, it was more of Ken's hype. Strike two.

It appeared clear, only to me, I guess, that Steve was not qualified to look after our complex high transaction volume projects. Ken would argue that hiring Steve would be much better than our status quo. Apparently, Steve's combination of business and technology expertise was a better fit than Maxine's purely financial background to establish and maintain control over projects. So, now Ken was also an ERCOT expert on internal controls? I could see Sam and Margaret missing that point, but shame on Tom for not catching it.

It was a typical corporate power grab that sometimes could result in something more sinister. If Ken wanted to exploit The Stakeholders' Golden Rule, Steve was as good as anyone to do it—holding out for the best result for Texans with unlimited project funding, no hard deadlines, and no pressure for results. It was a huge opportunity for fraud or other financial wrongdoings. The more I thought about it, the more it made sense: Steve was a perfect shill. Where did Steve come from?

Ken worked swiftly and effectively selling Steve to the officers and hyping his arrival with stakeholders. He emphasized our not only critical but also urgent need for a technology-savvy caretaker of project funding and project progress. Legislators, the Public Utility Commission staff, and stakeholders wanted it. With legislators appearing to be calling for more technology expertise, most of our board of directors had expected us to place more under technology control sooner rather than later. I was the only officer voicing opposition. It made me appear as a management problem rather than a management solution. Of course, this resulted in Ken painting another negative picture of me as divisive. He would have a talk with Tom about that to make sure Tom got an accurate take on that picture.

Ken made a big deal of the need to hire Steve without delay, as Steve was courting other opportunities. We had to make him a big offer ASAP or we would lose him. We were two days from year end, and Steve would no longer be available after December 31.

Gary Stroud, our woefully conscientious human resources director, brought up the fact that a background check was needed prior to any new hire, the idea apparently being that not having background information was the same as a bad reference. It should also be noted that Steve hadn't come to us through a recruiter, so we had no third party to rely on for a background check. As it turned out, Gary was never able to obtain any background information about Steve. There were no responses from Steve's references, and there wasn't enough time to make additional calls to get it done. That was strike three. We didn't know it at the time, but ERCOT had just struck out.

So, we hired Steve on December 31. Ironically, he occupied the office next to Gary. It was a daily reminder of the railroad job that took place to bring in Steve. For Gary, it must have been like a bad rash that wouldn't heal, likely knowing he would be the first person fired if something went wrong with Steve's job performance. I think Gary sensed something bad on the horizon from the moment Steve signed his employment agreement, but he couldn't do anything about it. Surely, people would understand that he didn't have enough time to do a background check.

16

Truth, Integrity, Trust, and Honor

December 2002 in Austin was a little cooler than Sue and I expected. Strong winds created quite a chill. We even had a few days of snow, which was totally unexpected, and, as we were told, quite unusual. The freeways and access roads iced over, keeping us stuck at home for two days. We were assured, again, that this was not really an Austin thing.

Our move from Atlanta had already run into some bumps and potholes. An offer to buy our house fell through. In addition, the bad weather in Austin delayed the start of construction of the new house we planned to build. We were almost back to square one on our move. We had a backup plan but had hoped we wouldn't have to use it. The whole month was a little chaotic for us.

Stakeholder activities at ERCOT slowed down a bit in December. It gave us a break from the politics, or so I thought. In fact, there was much more political activity during that first December than just the hiring of Steve Wallace.

Ken knew how to win over his following. We had only one official ERCOT December holiday event for all employees. Ken, however, created a second event, by invitation only. He took it upon himself to treat his staff and others he handpicked from across the company to his own private, white glove holiday dinner at a posh local restaurant. You were essentially staff royalty if you were invited. He handed out five-inch-tall stone pyramid party favors. The four sides of the pyramids were engraved with Truth, Integrity, Trust, and Honor. I was not one of the invitees.

I found out about the pyramid party favors from one my managers who had been invited. He said, "The people attending the dinner were quite impressed. The food was great. The white glove service made us all feel pretty important. The stone pyramids were awesome. Ken knows how to throw a party." I told him it was nice for Ken to invite him. I then asked if Ken's wife made it to the party. He said, "Ken told us that she couldn't make it." I wondered if she was still in jail in Dallas.

My manager went on to tell me that it was a department celebration Ken paid for out of his own pocket. He said, "Ken must have dug pretty deep in his pocket to pay that bill!"

Whoops! That couldn't be right. No way Ken paid for it out of his own pocket, so where did he get the money? The officers had no budget allocation for such events. The source of the funding never came up, but at our next executive committee meeting, Tom asked all of us to not do something like that again.

I never thought about hosting a holiday party. I was still living in a temporary apartment and trying to sell my house in Atlanta. Sue was flying back and forth. We were monitoring our spending to stay within the ERCOT relocation allowance. We spent a few days in Atlanta for Christmas, and that was it. Ebenezer Scrooge would have approved.

My staff settled for a "Secret Santa" exchange of small gifts in the office and a holiday potluck dinner gathering at the house of my executive assistant, Kerry Wariner. Kerry was the perfect executive assistant for me. All real, no bullshit. She was confident, fearless, and outspoken, in addition to being smart, honest, and hardworking. A fair-complexioned redhead, she had the fire in her eyes to match her hair. Thirty, with a robust build, she and her husband didn't have kids yet, but they had plans for a family. Kerry knew everybody at ERCOT, and everyone knew her. She was respected and plugged in tightly to company rumors. Sue and Kerry really got along well, and they would remain good friends even after I left ERCOT.

Sue and I brought a dish to Kerry's potluck dinner. Some people brought their kids, as it was more of a family event than a business affair. I'm sure my staff enjoyed the party, but it did make me feel inadequate when discussions touched on Ken's white glove restaurant event.

Back at ERCOT, the pyramids showed up on a lot of desktops. It was the Ken Shoquist code of "Truth, Integrity, Trust, and Honor." I thought those pyramids could have represented only one of two things. The holders of the pyramids were either part of a fantastic team building effort or part of an elaborate scam building effort. It seemed to me that, for them, it was just like the question of "Where did Ken get the money for his party?" It didn't matter. They were proud to be able to show off their pyramids.

Ken took an uncharacteristic wayward shot to win me over. He took me to dinner and suggested we get together weekly to work out at a fitness center. "We should talk on a more regular basis in a less formal setting," he said. "They have a great deal for new members at my gym."

That kind of bonding activity was a little too personal for me. I wouldn't bite. I told him that my days as a gym rat were way behind me. I suggested that it would be more productive for us to simply chat at dinner from time to time.

We coexisted without incident while the "business versus technology" elephant in the room feasted on the tension between us. I remained skeptical of Ken. His attempt to bond with me felt more like the early stages of a confidence game than sincere bonding. He showed no interest in what I thought were his core responsibilities. He proposed no material improvements in information technology maintenance and support. He offered nothing new for our retail market project, although he never missed an opportunity to remind people that it was all about technology glitches.

I stuck to my guns: performance was more important than politics. Ken was accumulating political capital at a feverish pace with no end in sight. Perhaps he would never have to show any results. I couldn't control that outcome, so I never complained about what I perceived as Ken's lackluster efforts to perform.

He continued to meet frequently with Tom to discuss further expansion of his duties, convincing Tom that he could handle it. He pointed out that most chief information officers had such expanded responsibilities. There would be no pushback from Sam, Margaret, or Maxine. I imagined that Ken might tell Tom something like this: "Board members likely expect the more up-to-date approach of expanded chief information officer responsibilities.

Ray just doesn't get it, and I'm hearing that he and his staff are getting harder to work with."

I had a good excuse to push back on Ken's "technology first" approach. The lessons learned from the late 1990s technology frenzy was still fresh in my mind. It's all about what business you are in, not the technology.

In addition, I had missed his dinner where he talked about Truth, Integrity, Trust, and Honor.

17

Foundation Work

Let me give you a reference point to better understand the context of this chapter:

In his book, *Confessions of a Confidence Man* (Sunwise Books: Middleton, WI, 2020), Edward H. Smith lists the "six definite steps or stages of growth" of a confidence game. He notes that the first stage is foundation work, where preparations are made in advance of the game, including the hiring of any assistants required and studying the background knowledge needed for the role.

I wouldn't dare share all my thoughts with anyone, but that is where my head was with all things related to Ken. His actions fit too perfectly into my obsession with what I saw as his potential conspiracy building.

Ken continued to move forward without any noticeable constraints. He had the confidence and the enthusiastic support of stakeholders and of Tom, Sam, and Margaret. In addition to Steve Wallace, he added two new lieutenants—Chris Uranga and

Kevin Judice. Handpicked by Ken, those three lieutenants (Steve included) enjoyed an almost free reign under Ken's umbrella. A new manager, Chris Douglas, who worked for Uranga as a database expert, enjoyed similar protection.

By spring 2003, Ken was on a roll. Shortly after the beginning of the new year, his domain expanded to include the construction of the second new 85,000-square-foot building in Taylor. Sam's staff that had built the first building were moved under Ken to build the second building. Maintenance and support of both the Taylor buildings would be under Ken as well. Contracts rolled in under his approval. I had no reason to believe that people moved from Sam's staff to Ken's staff would buy in to any wrongdoings, but there would be a whole lot of money going into that 85,000-square-foot building that would no longer be going through Sam's approval.

We needed that new building in Taylor. It was designed to be about the same size as the first building but with different features. There was no NASA-like control center—only office space and conference rooms. It was always part of the original ERCOT plan for all of Sam's, Ken's, and my operation activities to be based in Taylor.

My staff needed the space. We were working in ad hoc space that came available from time to time within Sam's and Ken's allocations in the first building in Taylor. Some of my staff temporarily occupied vacant cubicles and offices that were tagged for Sam's and Ken's future hires. Our retail market overhaul operation was housed mostly in retail space in a rundown strip shopping mall in Taylor. It wasn't safe there in the early morning hours or after dark. My staff working in the strip mall said that they didn't mind it, but

I knew they did. The second new building in Taylor would be used primarily to house all of my activities.

I believe Ken leveraged his responsibility for the new building to promote a savior-like façade. He was going to get Ray (me) and his staff the work environment they needed. It would have plenty of space, including a large breakroom area with assorted vending machines, microwave ovens, sink, and refrigerator. Twenty tables that each sat four made it feel like a cafeteria—not quite a Horn & Hardart automat, but functional enough for a cup of coffee, snack, or light lunch. Small groups could meet there to reduce the current excess demand for meeting rooms. If you had any suggestions for additional features, just ask Ken. He would take care of everything.

With his new construction responsibility, Ken was also able to get local officials to drink his Kool-Aid. His masterful dealing with local officials and politicians made him quite popular with them. He said he negotiated a property tax break for ERCOT, but, as far as I know, nobody confirmed it. That became an ERCOT standard procedure. Nobody ever confirmed his assertions, from what I could tell. Ken had to know it. Millions of dollars went through Ken for the construction. Everybody trusted Ken to know every contractor and how every penny was spent. I was certain he did. I was only concerned about whether or not those expenditures were solely related to ERCOT.

Tom seemed certain that Ken was totally legit. He handed off even more responsibility to Ken. At our second management committee meeting in February, Tom announced that he had expanded Ken's domain to company-wide physical security. Cybersecurity was already one of his duties, which could be leveraged to fortify the monitoring capabilities of our physical facilities. Physical security also fit with Ken's responsibilities for construction of the new building in Taylor as well as the maintenance and support of both buildings. Ken promised complete security coverage to protect against any attempted breach.

He jokingly said that would include monitoring restrooms. I wasn't sure it was a joke. Such activities were becoming a hobby for some very sick people using new video and internet technologies. It was an invasion of privacy showing up as entertainment content on some internet sites. I never saw one of those cameras at ERCOT, but I knew they now could be the size of a screw on the lock of the door. Could he be that sick? Wireless technology would take care of the communication with our master server to distribute pictures worldwide.

What was wrong with me? How could I think of such a thing? There was zero hard evidence of any wrongdoing. I was connecting dots of suspicion that were hearsay and circumstantial to create my own dark picture of Ken in my mind's eye. I became a little paranoid thinking that those dark thoughts were becoming too noticeable to others. I told myself that it was only the "business versus technology" elephant in the room, though I contemplated asking my doctor about an "anti-obsession with Ken" prescription. It would just be my luck. My doctor would probably tell me he knows Ken and, like his other friend, Ferris Bueller, that he is a really good guy.

In any event, trips to the restroom were never the same.

Chris Uranga was Ken's operations lieutenant. He was assigned the new responsibility for security. Thirty-seven years old, he looked much younger. His crew cut looked like it was a fresh cut every day, and his military-like behavior made it feel like you should salute him when you approached him and when he finished talking with you. I had to give Ken credit. His players looked like perfect fits for their roles.

Ken and Chris brought in an FBI agent to speak to ERCOT stakeholders about security. The agent looked like Chris right down to the crew cut. I was surprised that the FBI would allow this type of discussion in the first place. I resisted the thought that he might be Chris's brother. The FBI agent turned out to be a former, not current, FBI agent. Well, not exactly a former FBI agent, but he had worked in security with the federal government a few years earlier. This guy was impressive and really looked the part, much like all of Ken's confidants.

The alleged agent explained that physical security of grid operators was not a big concern. The lights going out was baked into most contingency plans of American businesses. They were equipped to handle outages. And a little paid time off didn't terrorize anyone. Cybersecurity was their biggest concern. They trusted NERC as the frontline entity to establish standards to cover that base.

Of course, Ken assured the stakeholders that he was working closely with Sam and had it all under control. He now had both physical and cybersecurity responsibilities. Chris was charged with keeping ERCOT up to date with NERC, the FBI, and other security agency recommendations. Nobody had the interest or the time to test him. They just believed him. It instantly increased their confidence in Ken's leadership.

It was another truckload of political capital to add to his stockpile. Yet, I couldn't see where he had produced any results. Could it be that my view of performance being more important than politics was not applicable in a quasi-governmental environment? It sure looked like it right now. Ken had achieved star status without any performance, in my opinion. He had established the foundation for his plan. Virtually all ERCOT capital spending was under his control.

The situation had me talking to myself: "Wait and see. You are right; performance trumps politics. He will have to perform at some point. Jim and Rich agree with you. Your staff is doing a great job. By the way, when did you start worrying so much about something totally out of your control? That's not like you."

At least I had someone to talk to, even if it was only myself.

A few months later, Ken told the management committee that he was reviewing the current contract with our outsourced physical security service. Their performance was only marginally acceptable. The contract was too expensive in light of their marginal performance. He had been in touch with a few firms that would be a better fit to meet our needs. One could provide much better service and save us some money. Chris Uranga and one of his new managers, Chris Douglas, were looking into the opportunity.

Great, but who cares?

We didn't need a new security contractor. In fact, all of the ERCOT staff liked those people and believed that they did a good job. I thought that with the change of the security contractor, Ken might be getting a little sloppy. He usually only targeted ERCOT's clearly basic needs. I'd have to see how his new security group idea plays out.

18
Wile E. Coyote

After months of temporary townhouse living while at ERCOT, Sue I and moved into our new house in May 2003.

It was a great sanctuary in a new subdivision just outside of Austin—a big (Texas-size), open floor plan right on the tenth fairway of a well-kept golf course. I could walk to the clubhouse to play or just hit some balls on the driving range. We were near three top-notch elementary schools where Sue qualified to substitute teach. The location was beautiful. Except for the occasional hail and tornado scare, the weather was great almost year-round.

Living in Austin was all about being outside. Golf and long walks were part of our weekly routine. Deer were everywhere, including in our front yard at night. Nothing scared them. They loved Sue's flowers, even those that were advertised as deer proof.

The first two years we were there, Dennis Quaid sponsored a celebrity golf tournament at our golf course. He was from Houston, but he had ties to Austin. Parts of his film *The Rookie* were shot in

Taylor. Quaid's celebrity tournament was fun. The host and most celebrities graciously stopped to pose for pictures during their round. Not many big names among them, but still, they were celebrities willing to give their time for a good cause. We could watch the players from our back porch but made sure we still paid admission as our contribution.

We were on the edge of what was called the Hill Country. Having lived only in the eastern U.S., we finally got to live around cactus, armadillos, and longhorn steers. The only downsides were the snakes and the vultures.

It was an eerie sight to see a flock of vultures feasting on a dead deer until they had picked it clean. They sat around the carcass in a pretty big group. A single deer would attract five or more for the feast. You knew they owned that deer. They gave you a menacing look when you drove by. It was a bit too graphic—a gruesome depiction of a part of the circle of life. Since Austin had an excess population of deer, that scene was pretty common.

I didn't realize how scary vultures really were until one set its sights right on me. One morning, I saw a dead cat in the street in front of our house. I put it in a box with the intent to later bury it by a creek or a group of cedar trees. I placed the box on top of our trash bin outside our garage. A short time after that, I went outside to get the mail and move the trash bin to the street. A huge vulture was perched on top of the box. It seemed a lot bigger than those I saw eating deer along the road. I guess being only a few feet away gave me a more accurate reading as to their size.

Treating it like it was just another bird, I approached it expecting it to fly away in fear. Instead, it sat up a little taller and stared at me. It was intimidating, and, as the nature of the confrontation began to sink in, it seemed to grow to be about five times larger than the vultures I had seen from a distance.

There was no question that it was I who was afraid. This was no mindless, feathered friend. This was a headstrong scavenger right on top of my trash can, and I had its dead cat. Getting what was rightfully his or hers was a matter of life or death. That seemed unreasonably harsh to me, but the vulture clearly was in no mood to negotiate. It was focused on me and our situation. I could almost hear it say, while sneering, "Go ahead, punk, make my day." It gave me a clear understanding of what a food fight must have meant to prehistoric beasts. I backed up and ran into the house.

The vulture eventually got tired of waiting for the lid of the box to open and decided to move on to a more readily available meal. At least I was able to give the cat a respectable burial in the woods.

Even though Sue and I had moved into the house, our builder was working on the repair glitches in the construction of our new house. The punch list was short, but the problems, no matter how small, needed to be fixed.

Our house had a covered patio with a built-in brick natural gas grill, which we couldn't get lit. It wasn't a punch list item, so Sue called our builder to have someone come over to check it out.

There seemed to be something wrong with the natural gas feed to the burners. The builder's assistant tried to light it a number of times but couldn't get it to work. He did smell gas but got no flame. His thinking was to look for any obvious outside problems along the gas pipe before calling the gas company. He walked around the grill down the side of the house looking for the control for the natural gas feed.

Rather than leaving it up to the builder's assistant, Sue decided to help. She thought that he might not have gotten close enough for the gas to catch a flame. I never liked her comfort level when tending to those things. Pilot lights and gas oven burners never seemed to scare her. She took a fireplace lighter and stuck her head into the grill to get close.

There was a loud explosion. The builder's assistant ran down the side of the house and around to the grill to see what happened. He took one look at Sue and ran away.

Sue was stunned. She went inside and looked in the mirror. Her eyebrows were singed. Her hair was blown out into all directions and singed on the ends. Her face was blackened with soot. She said she looked like Wile E. Coyote after receiving a package—marked "Acme," of course—containing a bomb from the Roadrunner. "Meep! Meep!"

Sue called me to come home right away. She said she was okay, but there was a house issue I needed to look at without delay. When I got there, she was laughing. She said, " It blew up, then the builder's assistant took one look at me and ran away!" She said that three guys on the golf course heard the explosion and came over to investigate. They had the same reaction. "They took one look at me, and they quickly rode off in their golf carts."

Sue was not hurt. No burns, cuts, or bruises. She had cleaned up before I got there and looked fine. Her face was a little red and the singed eyebrows were an obvious result from the blast.

I didn't see any damage to the grill, the patio, or the outside of our house, either, although all that was secondary to Sue's well-being. There was no damage to the kitchen that backed up to the patio. I then checked upstairs. One bedroom was on the back wall above the kitchen. What I saw was incredible. That back wall of the bedroom above the kitchen had blown out. A tall heavy chest had fallen over from the blast. It wasn't a small flare-up. It was a *blast*. I couldn't believe Sue hadn't been hurt.

Sue kept telling me how funny it was when the first guy looked at her and ran away. I didn't want to laugh, but it *was* funny. The picture in my mind's eye was too vivid. Sue was just being Sue.

"Meep! Meep!"

19

The Politics of Change

From the beginning of the year through the spring of 2003, ERCOT activities, outside of Ken's expanding responsibilities, remained pretty much the same. We were all staying in our lanes. I had my people focused on our job. Sam had his people focused on their job. Maxine and Margaret's finance and administration teams focused on their jobs. Everybody appeared to be doing what they were told.

Stakeholders were happy. They even stopped giving me agita for a while as their attention shifted to the increasing probability of an ERCOT wholesale market overhaul. Their attention shift was helpful to me and my peers because it redirected their passion about ERCOT to that debate and away from our current operations and the strict adherence to their instructions. Our effort to fix the retail market got some well-deserved breathing room.

The debate about the merits of an ERCOT wholesale market overhaul was in full swing. Remember, there was no legislation ordering an ERCOT wholesale market change. It was all about pressure from Washington, D.C. Under Pat Wood, the former head of the Texas Public Utility Commission, the Federal Energy Regulatory Commission had adopted new guidelines for the creation and operation of electric power grids.

The ERCOT business model did *not* conform to those guidelines, but we didn't have to conform because the Texas grid was exempt. As mentioned earlier, the fact that we were exempt from those federal guidelines became an issue. Politically, the president needed Texas to conform to further his deregulation agenda nationwide. There were five other electric power pool grids that already conformed to the new federal guidelines. They were used as examples for how Texas should conform. Despite our exemption, the politics associated with our Texas favorite son in the White House urged our compliance.

The first hurdle was by far the highest. Whether or not an overhaul of the ERCOT wholesale market was right for Texans took center stage.

There was an attempt to take the federal politics out of the debate. Favorite son as American president or not, the last thing Texas would do was to change to conform with federal guidelines that had no jurisdiction over their activity. ERCOT did not *have* to change. It would only do so if it made sense for Texans.

Of course, there wasn't a snowball's chance in hell that politics would be ignored for any decision in the ERCOT quasi-governmental environment. Stakeholders went on record with their individual positions on the matter through their testimony at the Public Utility Commission. But the politics were in play without any Public Utility Commission testimony. They carried as much, if not more, weight than the stakeholders' testimony.

The debate immediately started out in the weeds. The initial lead complaint about ERCOT's wholesale market was the current ERCOT resolution of network bottlenecks, referred to as "grid congestion." Complex detailed arguments were presented to show that the subjective resolution of congestion by ERCOT was *too* subjective and did not yield the best result. Those arguments concluded that an objective, automated solution, like one used at other grid operators, should be implemented to obtain the optimal result.

The complaints about congestion drew a lot of attention but were really a red herring. Everyone knew it. Proponents for change had trouble making their grid congestion point. It became an argument with a fatal flaw. It went something like this: "You just don't understand how the grid works—it's rocket science. With an automated solution, the grid operation will be more reliable."

More reliable? Nobody would testify to that. If Sam believed that, it would have been done that way in the original implementation. It was generally agreed that an automated resolution of congestion might make ERCOT's job easier, but that was about it. Without improving reliability, the automated resolution of congestion argument became irrelevant.

The real ERCOT wholesale market issue had to do with bundled bids and bundled dispatch of groups of generating units. The large incumbent generators and public power municipal and cooperative utilities argued that bundling was a "must have" feature of the current ERCOT wholesale market. Independent generators and energy marketers argued that bundled bids and dispatch were a major impediment to fair competition. Individual generating unit bids, not bundles, were essential to level the competitive playing field. Leveling the playing field was a much better case for change than the rocket science congestion argument, but it was supported only by those two stakeholder groups.

Federal politics came back into play. Current ERCOT protocols allowing bundled bids were contrary to the new federal deregulation guidelines. The cornerstone of those guidelines was the concept of individual generating unit bids, not bundles. The difference between the federal guidelines and the ERCOT wholesale market design crept back into the case for change. Independent generators and energy marketers exploited the politics by arguing that competition in Texas would be significantly enhanced by Texas compliance with the federal guidelines.

Other complex issues also pushed the debate in many different directions. It was up to the three Texas public utility commissioners to decide what ERCOT should do. The challenge boiled down to the current thinking of each of those three commissioners. They were appointed by the governor instead of being elected by the general population. That—unfortunately, in my opinion—minimized the desires of consumers. Consumers were only part of the retail market and not a participant in the ERCOT wholesale market. The consumer stakeholder group representatives certainly understood the problem but contributed no relevant input to the technical and political debates, other than their concerns about the complexity and possible unacceptable cost to make a change.

The commissioners had to decide whether or not they should initiate a rulemaking procedure for an ERCOT wholesale market change. There was the compelling argument presented by the independent generator and energy marketer stakeholder groups for a revolutionary change to attain pure competition between generating units and not just between generation company bundles. Incumbent generators argued that a middle ground of evolutionary change would make the most sense. The municipal and cooperative utilities, however, were against any change. They argued that their public power agreements with their customers required their generation be bundled specifically for those public power customers. From what I could see, the industrial consumer, commercial consumer, and residential consumer stakeholder groups were against any change.

It couldn't get much better than this. One commissioner was for change, one was against it, and one was "on the fence." Finally, we had some entertainment outside the walls of ERCOT. The commissioners were lobbied by just about every constituent telling them what they wanted, and I had a front-row seat to see how real political appointees deal with a no-win situation. The only downside was that we couldn't bring popcorn into the Public Utility Commission hearing room.

The chairperson of the commission was still Becky Klein, who apparently believed that the argument for a more level playing field was too strong to ignore. She also wanted to help out the Texas favorite son, Bush the younger, in the White House. She was all in for change.

The commissioner who was against change was the most tenured and always looked the most frustrated. Brett Perlman was a nice fellow with the courage to stick to his convictions. The daily political grind had seemingly taken its toll on Brett, who was more gray-haired than you might expect for someone in his mid-forties. He had only a year remaining to serve, and beyond that he was unlikely to have any political influence once he retired from the commission.

Brett had a pre-deregulation view of his role as a commissioner. Before deregulation, the public utility commissioners were consumer-oriented. There was no wholesale competition. It was all about what end use consumers would pay for electricity. He believed that, despite all the food fights over wholesale market competition, it was still about consumers. They didn't want a change to the ERCOT wholesale market. Neither did Brett.

That put the third commissioner in a tough situation. Based on what she was saying, Julie Parsley, a proud Texas A&M alum probably in her mid-thirties and the newest appointee to the commission, was on the fence, neither for nor against an ERCOT wholesale market change.

Julie was smart and obviously politically astute to have been selected for such a difficult position. What surprised me about her was her being on the fence. I assumed that as the most recent appointee, she, like Becky, would be all in on change. I guess the governor wanted to be sure that we didn't lose sight of the pride associated with being the Lone Star State.

Julie's "on the fence" position kept the ERCOT wholesale market overhaul debate lively and its outcome clearly uncertain. It dragged out the timeline too. The three commissioners came to a politically acceptable decision: "Let's study it a little more," they said. Cost/benefit was a shared concern, so they ordered a cost/benefit study.

All of the stakeholders knew that any result of such a study would be based on only one set of assumptions that could be contested ad nauseum. That is exactly what happened. There were too many variables. Too many assumptions. The easy and often-used argument of "garbage in, garbage out" overshadowed the results. The study was deemed inconclusive.

As the debates continued, the biggest issue became a bit disturbing to me. Per my assessment, the residential consumer stakeholder group didn't want a change. Ditto the industrial consumer stakeholder group, the commercial consumer stakeholder group, the municipal public power utilities stakeholder group, and the cooperative public power utilities stakeholder group. No, no, no, no, no. Basically, Texas consumers just didn't want it.

With a 2-to-1 vote, the commissioners approved the motion to change the ERCOT wholesale market. Seriously, what business in its right collective mind does something that its customers *don't* want? If ERCOT was not a quasi-governmental entity, there would be no ERCOT wholesale market overhaul.

20

Carpe Diem

The floodgates opened. The next step was for the commissioners to construct and issue their rule for the change. It would include another round of lobbying and hearings. Battle lines were drawn by the stakeholder groups for a white-collar Texas civil war. All stakeholders were energized. Some groups geared up to completely replace all current wholesale market protocols. Some groups mobilized to ensure minimum change. There was even some activity to put together an appeal to revisit the no-change option.

Whatever the preference, there was a groundswell of stakeholder activity. Meetings and more meetings. The ERCOT wholesale market overhaul project had all the makings of a perfect storm. It required a quasi-governmental totally stakeholder-driven, all-inclusive process. It also was in lockstep with The Stakeholders' Golden Rule. There would be no time or money constraints. How could any ship navigate through that storm to get anything done?

Stakeholders lobbied each other. They lobbied the commissioners. They even lobbied legislators to help push their agenda. They met. They voted within their groups. They met some more. The quasi-governmental environment enabled everybody to be adequately informed and to participate. ERCOT officers simply waited to be told what to do. We could watch as long as we kept quiet. We weren't going to get fired for that.

We stayed busy minding our own business in our lanes. Rich Gruber's stakeholder services group provided outstanding administrative support as needed for any special meetings related to the commissioners' ERCOT wholesale market overhaul rulemaking process. Jim Galvin's group kept their heads down making significant progress on the retail market problems. Sam Jones was called on occasionally by the Public Utility Commission staff and stakeholder groups to address any possible grid reliability issues that came up during the rulemaking debates. Tom Noel proclaimed that we would do whatever it might take to implement the details of any protocol changes approved by stakeholders.

Ken was as happy as a pig in shit with the commissioners' decision to overhaul the ERCOT wholesale market. He saw opportunity. He was already motivated to profit from the new Texas civil war. His challenge was to figure out the means to make it happen. His thinking was far more sophisticated than that of a carpetbagger. With Ivar Kreuger-like confidence and sweet-talking aplomb (referring to the Swedish "Match King" of the early twentieth century), Ken set up a mission critical project to explore the ERCOT technology requirements for the overhaul.

Steve Wallace was assigned to manage that mission critical technology research project. To make sure Ken didn't miss anything, the project would consider all the "technology what-ifs" of a complete ERCOT wholesale market replacement. We had to be ready for the biggest and the best for Texans. In keeping with The Stakeholders' Golden Rule, Steve's project had no budget or completion date. Tasks would be defined on an as-needed basis. Depending on the amount of any individual expenditure, disbursements would be approved by either Steve or Ken.

With misguided confidence in Ken, Tom thought that the project made sense. So did Sam and Margaret. The project appeared harmless to them. Maxine and I were the only skeptics. Why start a new technology project we didn't need? The other ERCOT officers expected that point of view from Maxine and me. Tom considered our concerns but allowed Ken to proceed.

Every project had to have a cost estimate in order to be allocated capital funds. Ken and Steve thought that two million dollars would be a good starting point for their technology research project. Ken said something about not wanting to take a "do-nothing" stance that he described as "prehistoric," complete with dinosaurs. As best as I can recall, he said, "We need to be ready to meet stakeholder technology needs. Failing to do so is how we got in the 'retail market quagmire.' We don't want to repeat that mistake." That said, Tom, Sam, and Margaret thought that Ken's technology research project made even more sense. It was the means for Ken to exploit the opportunity.

Ken brought in a new advisor based in Boston for his new technology project. It seemed strange that he didn't have the recognizable Boston accent; instead, this guy had a "totally lost" air about him, even though Ken presented him as a business expert with superior economic expertise and extensive experience in energy markets.

Stakeholders I talked to had never heard of this guy. No one on ERCOT's staff had ever heard of him. The Public Utility Commission staff didn't know who he was, and he had no Texas legislature ties. He wasn't brought in as an employee, so, as far as I know, nobody ever saw a resume. Wow.

I was never asked to interview him. Of course, I had him pegged as a phony. He would have to live up to his hype for me to think anything different. But I had no reason to object to him joining the team. Margaret put together his consulting contract and never raised any red flags.

Steve and Chris knew him pretty well. I assumed this might just be Ken continuing to get his old gang back together for this Austin gig. Our so-called Boston guy never met with any other ERCOT officers or stakeholders. He talked only to Ken, Steve, Chris, and a few other information technology people. I think Ken instructed him to avoid businesspeople to make sure he wouldn't be unmasked. It was a wise move on his part—he was such a ghost that I regularly forgot his name.

Ken said we wouldn't see him at the office very much because he was out on assignments. Nobody outside my team questioned what he was doing. It amazed me that such a high-priced ghost could get security clearance with a free rein within our facility. Oh, yeah: Ken was in charge of security.

Ken was approaching a political capital stash even greater than Sam's! His new technology project included anything he deemed necessary to ultimately satisfy stakeholders. He used the project to explore the boundaries of the ERCOT wholesale market overhaul project opportunity.

He saw that the ERCOT wholesale market overhaul was likely to have a significant federal government influence. He recognized that other ERCOT-like entities had an interest in having ERCOT conform with their design. Why not tie the ERCOT wholesale market overhaul into a single national project? That could get all the nationwide grid operations on exactly the same page enabling nationwide electricity commodity competition. A national project to research that possibility, headed by Steve, might make sense to Ken's peers at the five other ERCOT-like entities.

We all traveled periodically across the country to ERCOT-related industry events. Sam had his NERC meetings. I met with market operations officers of the other grid operators. Ken met with his peers as well. He used those meetings to talk with them about his idea.

One afternoon, I received a call from Bill Workman, my counterpart at the PJM power pool. They were the premier grid operator in the country . . . other than Texas, of course. They managed a multistate grid long before the deregulation movement. They were generally considered the gold standard of grid operators by the Federal Energy Regulatory Commission. It was just a short train ride from their office outside of Philadelphia to federal offices in Washington, D.C. It naturally followed that they were used as the business model for establishing the new federal deregulation guidelines.

It was also well known around the country that most of our Texas constituents didn't care about the federal standard. Our peers around the country always expected us to do things our own way. Any appearance of conforming activities would be a surprise.

Bill was angry. He asked, "What the hell is going on down there?" I said, "Things are great. The cattle are gaining weight, the corn crop had one of its highest yields ever this year, the cotton fields are snowy white and ripe for pickin', and, last I heard, crude prices are up." He wasn't amused. He asked, "Why are you proposing to bring together the power pools to create a national platform based on the new Texas model?"

Ken had stirred up the pot testing the boundaries of his opportunity. I knew he could never make that happen, but I wasn't surprised that it might have made sense to some of his information technology brethren around the country to start a research project. Running it up the flagpole was quintessential Ken.

I told Bill not to worry: "We have a chief information officer run amok. A national project has never entered anybody's mind down here. We have a big enough challenge with just a Texas project. We have enough on our plate right now."

Bill still wasn't happy, but he understood. He had been through the whole "business versus technology" thing. That elephant in the room left their building a few years earlier after they upgraded their systems.

Ken was quite a character—brilliantly blending motive, means and opportunity. Carpe diem run amok.

21
Just a Misunderstanding

Dracula and his team controlled the blood bank. Ken controlled virtually all of ERCOT capital spending as well as his swollen operating budget. His control of the technology research project for the ERCOT wholesale market overhaul got most of my attention. Steve managed it. Using what I saw as Ken's expert talents to deceive, he successfully avoided any effort to audit their work. Ken also controlled construction of the second 85,000-square-foot building in Taylor. He also controlled physical security at both Taylor and our Austin headquarters. All of the work on all three efforts was performed by outside consultants. By contracting with outside firms for the work, Ken had opportunities to take blood from all three of those sources. From a Dracula perspective, Ken, Steve, and Chris were all blood type AB+. They were compatible with any transfusion of cash. Any blood type would do.

Tom simply gave Ken free rein. Sam was too busy "keeping the lights on" to be concerned with Ken. Maxine dutifully accounted for the contract activity. She worried, as was the nature of a chief financial officer, but stayed in her lane. Margaret generated the contracts. She still held fast to the technology-first approach. She stuck to her guns to process contracts as fast as Ken demanded. Her adherence to the quasi-governmental practice of restricted roles kept her working with blinders on, which continued to bother me.

I worried about the ultimate impact on me resulting from my tacit acceptance of their narrow focus. No fiduciary responsibility. No confirmation of work being done for a valid business purpose. Only legal matters to ensure contracts were enforceable. Only checks cut on demand as completed contract obligations were confirmed from Ken and Steve.

One day, one of Margaret's lawyers, Chip Weeden, who was on point for Ken's contracting, abruptly quit. Supposedly, he and Margaret didn't see eye-to-eye. Chip wasn't comfortable with Ken's urgency to push his contracts through with inadequate time for review. He was an old school corporate lawyer. Unfortunately for Chip, ERCOT was not a good place for a lawyer with a "for-profit" corporate contracting background. I thought he might have been the first to see black and white evidence of a contract with no apparent business purpose. He resigned to pursue other interests. I always suspected that Chip might have eventually played a role in the ERCOT saga similar to Watergate's "Deep Throat." I didn't know that for sure, but it would fit, if his conscience had gotten the best of him.

I kept reminding myself that, in this quasi-governmental structure, I had no fiduciary responsibility related to the actions of my peers. I stayed focused on the great strides we were making with our retail market work. For my team, Ken's shenanigans were just a nuisance that had become part of our daily routine. I still kept one eye on Ken.

Ken and Steve's project to research the information technology needs for the ERCOT wholesale market overhaul steadily grew in scope and dollars spent under the alleged urgent need for technology preparedness. Those two did have some results to show for it. Steve bought a big house on Lake Travis, and Ken treated himself to an expensive Mercedes. Steve assured stakeholders and our board of directors that he was on track with the ERCOT wholesale market technology preparedness project. He promised that the project would be completed on time, within the ERCOT wholesale market overhaul timeframe. In other words, in accordance with The Stakeholders' Golden Rule, pretty much never.

Ken and Steve even claimed to be providing the cornerstone work for the retail market fix. Jim and Rich went along with it, even though Ken and Steve were doing nothing for us. I couldn't complain. How could Dracula be at fault for anything when he was claiming to be doing everything right? He could only be caught if he was actually doing something wrong. There was no hard evidence of that.

My MBA side had to give Ken credit. With a long-term strategy to expand to a nationwide wholesale market platform development effort, he created a pretty effective Texas-based technology research operation.

Ken did stub his toe due to his aggressive hype to take charge of a nationwide wholesale market platform. He took a trip on his own to meet with APR Inc., the company that owned the application software that my group used for processing market settlements.

APR was a small boutique operation. They met a well-defined niche with a flexible and adaptable product. The cost of the license for our use of the APR software was reasonable. APR interfaced with both Jim's group and our pre-Ken information technology staff, and we had an excellent relationship with them through both groups. They licensed their platform to other ERCOT-like grid operators. Their application passed numerous tests at each entity. We planned to continue to use it for our portion of any ERCOT wholesale market overhaul settlement and billing needs.

Paul Singer was the hands-on owner of APR and managed his business relationships. He wanted to grow his business but was more interested in making sure APR didn't get spread too thin. Paul was a good small-businessman—the kind you liked to be dealing with to meet critical application software needs.

Paul had never met Ken prior to Ken's trip to meet with him. It seemed innocent enough; after all, our chief information officer should be in the loop with him. Ken initiated his discussion with Paul by teasing him about his ties with the information technology leaders of other ERCOT-like entities. He told him he was in charge of the review of a possible national platform.

Ken then flexed his muscles. He told Paul that he was now responsible for ERCOT's decision on software applications. We would need an APR-like application for the ERCOT wholesale market overhaul project. That decision would be his and his alone.

Paul soon found Ken to be anything but innocent. After those two had met, one of our staff members received a call from a consultant who had worked with us on the original implementation of the APR software. He said that Paul didn't appreciate the shakedown. Our staff member asked, "What shakedown are you talking about?" Apparently, Ken wanted a 5 percent interest in APR to allow Paul to keep working with ERCOT.

What would you do with that information? Go to Tom? Have Ken deny it? Drag in a vendor to help air your dirty laundry? Have all of that develop into a discussion of how it was all a misunderstanding? Ken would probably say something like, "I brought it up within the context of a 5 percent ERCOT interest, not a personal interest. Ray should not make accusations without knowing all the facts!" I decided to de-escalate and wait for something more tangible before saying anything to anyone.

Jim Galvin assured Paul that Ken did not speak for ERCOT. Jim told him, "We never had discussed with Ken any desire for a 5 percent interest in APR. Ken may have been trying to impress Tom Noel with his negotiation tactics. We have seen a lot of that lately. Ray will be taking care of it."

It went on my list of "suspicious hearsay items attributable to Ken's activities." I knew it was more than just a misunderstanding.

22
The Coincidence

The bug up my ass about Ken was taking up too much bandwidth in my brain—not to mention all the time I was spending talking to myself about his success with Tom, the other officers, and the stakeholders. I tried to go more often to a Happy Gilmore "happy place" of my own.

The Thursday afternoon ERCOT golf event was a pretty good escape. We would meet at the Taylor golf course, the "Old Course," as some referred to it, a nine-hole beauty carved into the hillside between two farms. The cattle gathered to watch us play. Trash talk and camaraderie highlighted the twilight nine-hole competition. The discussion at the end of the round focused on where we should go for a few beers. It would already be too late for dinner, so chips, dip, and beer would have to get us home. The golfing gang was a fun group. I was the only officer participant, but I never felt out of place.

The road home from Taylor ran past an ostrich farm. One time I stopped to observe their curious behavior. I never thought I'd see them outside of a zoo. I didn't get too close to them. They have quite a temper, so I had heard. There were holes in the ground. I guessed that was where they stuck their heads to hide from their owner. Anyway, seeing the ostrich farm on the road home from Taylor fit into my Thursday afternoon happy place.

I really enjoyed those Thursday afternoons, but they were never enough to steer totally clear of all things Ken. A much-longer break from the Ken shenanigans would have been nice but was not to be. When things seemed to quiet down, something new would pop up. He seemed to always be up to something odd.

My perception of Ken was as a master exploiter of basic human needs. You could be sure that, whatever he was up to, it was rooted in people believing in him. He was willing to go to great lengths to secure a personal bond with a key player. He wanted to be sure he could count on that player for support when needed, and nothing illegal about securing a personal bond. How Ken exploited that support was at his own discretion. He had set himself up to have the time and the money to add to his stockpile of political capital.

Ken took a few days off to travel to Latvia. He said he had relatives there whom he hadn't seen in a long time. During his visit, he happened to bump into Ted Jenkins, an officer at one of our stakeholder transmission and distribution stakeholder companies. Ted was **THE** key stakeholder representative for our retail market problem-solving activities. Ted was a wonderful man— open, honest, and caring. He had taken me under his wing shortly after I arrived at ERCOT. He also wanted to help us with the retail market challenge and was the stakeholder best positioned to do it. Ken knew all that.

Ted was on a ministry mission to Latvia through his church.

It was another piece to the puzzle. I found out about it through our grapevine of interesting information tidbits. It went something like this: Ted had just finished delivering a speech about his ministry when Ken emerged from the church crowd, and, according to Ted, what ensued went something like this: "What a coincidence!" Ken said. "I'm sitting here with my cousin and you stepped up to the podium. Great to see you! Your speech was inspiring! Thank you for your mission." They talked for a while until Ken was sure Ted was hooked on his sincerity.

Like Ted, Ken was also on a mission. It had nothing to do with a church ministry, but it did relate to tugging at a man's soul. He wanted Ted to see things his way. It didn't require any technical meetings. He would gain Ted's confidence the way he knew best—even at a church in Latvia.

I felt like it was a low blow, even by Ken's low standards. I don't know if Ted ever realized that his encounter with Ken had nothing to do with relatives or going to church. There was never any wrongdoing. Just some good old-fashioned bonding with Ken.

It was another entry to my growing list of "suspicious hearsay items attributable to Ken's activities."

23

Is That Man Ethical?

James Cohea was Jim Galvin's lead manager working with both his staff and stakeholders to pull the retail market out of the ditch. He was medium height and heavyset, in his mid-forties and seasoned, much like most people on my staff. He wore thick glasses, but you could still clearly see his eyes. They were constantly an indication that his brain was quickly and precisely processing information. Much like Jim, James was a grinder. Unfortunately, he was unaware that cancer was getting ready to take hold of him.

James was no ERCOT android. He didn't care much for ERCOT management. He had work to do, and he would do it his way. Attention to anything else was a waste of time. He was plugged into all staff-level rumors but retained only those that might impact his work. James was the expert on how it all fit together and what needed to be changed. The stakeholders working with him knew that about him, and they gave him a pass to tell them what needed to be done.

Ken's large staff took up so much office space that James's team had to work from some retail space we rented in that local strip mall I mentioned earlier. It didn't matter to James. He enjoyed being in the trenches, right where the rubber meets the road, so to speak. He needed no artificial prestige by being in a main building. Everybody knew who he was and how hard he worked.

James was open and honest with anyone fortunate enough to engage him in conversation. He wouldn't let his concerns or his staff's complaints fester. He readily shared those with Jim. He did respect the confidential nature of those exchanges with his staff. It would be unusual for James to bring up any such issues at a meeting with his fellow managers and me. But one time, he did.

We were in a meeting with Jim and Rich and their managers for a retail market project update. Maxine was there for the update as well. James looked preoccupied. Something was bothering him. As the discussion shifted to our interface with Ken's team, James couldn't sit still. He suddenly blurted out, "Is that man ethical?" I asked "Who?" He said, "Ken. Does he have any ethics at all?"

We agreed to address it after the meeting.

Jim and I met with James in private to drill down on his comment. It was clearly only about rumors and James's gut feelings. He said he had no hard evidence of wrongdoing, but he was getting complaints from his staff about the activities of Ken's lieutenants. "They spend too much time in closed-door meetings doing nothing of any value for ERCOT to show for it," James said. "A weekend junket to the Caribbean is apparently in the works. That guy from Boston doesn't do anything. A lot of money is flowing through the new ERCOT wholesale market technology research project. It just doesn't smell right."

I was certain that the stink was more than a little gas passed by the "business versus technology" elephant in the room. I was also certain that there wasn't anything we could do about it. We asked James to keep us posted. I now felt obligated, but only in a personal way, to watch Ken's moves a little closer. Professionally, I needed to stay in my lane. It was the only way I could go that would enable people to continue to confide in me.

From time to time, officers interviewed recruits for each other. A few days after hearing from James, I was asked by Kevin Judice to talk with Ben Gregory, a new software applications person to interact with my team. Ben was a nice guy. Confident, but not as cocky as most of Ken's staff.

On paper, Ben was well-qualified. Jim and James had already talked with him. They were okay with bringing him in. Our face-to-face meeting confirmed that he appeared to be a good fit. We talked shop for a while.

Ben was excited about the opportunity, especially since it paid a performance bonus. "Where did you hear that?" I asked. Before he could answer, I said, "We don't pay performance bonuses to staff." He said that was his original understanding, but Ken had told him that we did. He had confirmed it with Ken: "Ken told me it isn't standard, but he had ways to pay such bonuses outside our normal compensation process."

I paused and just looked at Ben. He turned a little red in the face realizing he had said something he shouldn't have. I didn't dispute Ken's promise of a bonus. It was a small piece of the puzzle that fit just right. I believed Ben was an honest guy. I never tagged him as an accomplice to any kind of wrongdoing.

After James's comments and my encounter with Ben, my interfaces with Ken became more strained. I was suffering from too many flashbacks to my old duties as a chief financial officer. There still wasn't anything to justify pushing the panic button, although it was getting harder to hide my feelings. Once you are bitten by the fiduciary responsibility bug, you never get over it.

The other officers could feel the tension growing between Ken and me, and they advised Tom to intervene. He decided to address it at my next performance review. The discussion was candid and respectable, and quite a bit strained. We both had some vetting on our mind. Tom told me that for him to keep me onboard, I needed to get along with Ken.

Still fresh in my mind, I shared James's concern and my conversation with Ben Gregory. Tom didn't blink. Ken had a much bigger stockpile of political capital than Tom. We both knew it. He reiterated the need for me to modify my behavior. I stood my ground, asking that he get a little closer to the details of Ken's activities.

Tom was a good man. You could count on him to listen and keep an open mind on all you had to tell him. I knew he felt I was honest and had hired me because of what he felt were superior business instincts. I was sharing some valuable information coming from those instincts.

Tom didn't comment further. He made his point but appeared a bit unsure. I guessed he might have been hearing other rumblings about Ken. Just like James, in the back of Tom's mind, the question haunted him: "Is that man ethical?"

24

Performance Beats Politics

My re-energized staff was focused on the retail market overhaul challenge. It was tempting to dive into the details; our firefighting mode took us there a lot. But this had to be different. It would be acceptable to revisit high-level assumptions to go down some new paths for analysis. We needed to examine the entire stakeholder process from the top down.

We started with what we knew best. It was that nagging six million-plus automated real-time usage meter thing that gave credence to the spin of a technology glitch. Legislators resisted any attempt at an explanation of or solution for the problem that was more than simply those two words—*technology glitch*. From their point of view, the retail market problem would always be ERCOT's inability to work with a simple solution using the latest technology. If *Guinness World Records* kept track of such things, it might have been the biggest technology glitch ever in the world.

The glitch spin was too simplistic and naïve. In fact, as we had tried to communicate over and over, it wasn't even a technology problem. It was a business problem and required a phased-in business effort over a number of years that had already been started by the transmission and distribution companies who would procure, operate, and maintain the new meters. Period.

Jim's surgical team was ready to operate. James was precise in his every move. His skills were superb as were those of his staff and the stakeholders' staffs. They did a masterful job coming up with solutions that the retail electric providers found acceptable. The plan was to complete the project in less than a year, including testing and full cut-over to enable daily switch transactions. The three- to-five-year phase-in of six million-plus automated meters would easily plug in to ultimately replace that retail market fix.

The information technology component was small compared to the business components. We identified the necessary computer code changes and file-processing changes.

The business changes were the biggest challenge. Retail electric providers had to develop new daily processes to take responsibility for the accuracy of daily switch input notices. The transmission and distribution companies had to develop new daily processes to ensure the timely receipt of those notices from retail electric providers and accept responsibility for the accuracy of the metered usage transmitted to ERCOT. Both stakeholder groups had to approve the upgraded daily load profile algorithms developed by our team. We also had to come up with what we called a stacking process to handle a new switch request for a single meter occurring within the time period between a previous switch request and the completion of that meter read. Both stakeholder groups approved that process as well.

During the project, Rich and his team did a great job keeping the retail market participants patient and upbeat. Jim and James and their team assured stakeholders that the retail market was going to survive and thrive. The only change that would be needed after this work was to install those millions of automated real-time usage meters and incorporate their readings into our system.

Not surprisingly, legislators continued to growl about why we hadn't made that happen yet. For them, it was still just a technology glitch to be fixed. They never let go of it no matter what anyone said to the contrary. Their lack of understanding and appreciation that there was probably a three- to-five-year effort involved to make it all happen was really annoying. They were certainly smart enough to get it. They didn't have the time or desire to try.

To add a little fuel to the fire, legislators were hearing a lot about the alleged retail market technology glitch from some ERCOT stakeholders who had gotten in the habit of bonding with legislators through their criticism of ERCOT. There was no stopping that, but I wished that those stakeholders, particularly those who knew better, would stop blowing in the legislators' ears.

There was one thirty-something stakeholder, Barbara Keener, representing retail electric providers who had a few key, older male legislators eating out of her hand. She always wore tight low-cut blouses and short dresses to let everyone know her lobbying efforts could never miss their target of getting the attention of the legislators.

Barbara was a leading spokesperson for the retail electric provider group. She was sharp enough to impress people without all the glitz. She and her husband had started a retail electric provider company. They established a solid business that outperformed most other small retailer electric providers. From her standpoint, installing all those automated real-time usage meters and reworking ERCOT systems was an old 1990s kind of technology problem that should have been addressed by ERCOT from their beginning. She knew it was a big effort but felt that the only way to get enough attention to fix the problem was to oversell an oversimplified spin centered on the concept of a technology glitch.

Fortunately, Barbara Keener was only an outlier when you looked at the entire retail electric provider group. All the other retail electric providers knew that we were doing exactly the right things and appreciated our work. Even though Barbara was competing with them every day, I wished she would have worked more in sync with all of her retail electric provider brethren for ERCOT issues.

We knew we were fixing the right problems with the right solutions and with all the right stakeholder participation. The changes we were making solved the problem and would pave the way for the technology desired by legislators to plug in seamlessly to what we put in place.

So many people were doing first-class work on an incredibly complex business problem. There was a quiet confidence now evidenced in discussions between all of our staff and stakeholders.

It was all about performance beating politics. We knew we would get it right.

DERELICTION

25
Tip of the Iceberg

Have you ever met a part-time actor working as a security guard? There is probably some of that in Hollywood. It might not be unusual in Austin, either. Except when they show up as a security guard under a contract negotiated by Ken.

Carlos Luquis was pretty smooth. He was the contracted lieutenant under Chris Uranga for the new ERCOT physical security team. Ken assured ERCOT that Carlos would bring in a new facilities security team based in San Antonio. They would be at least as good as and more economical than the existing team. As promised, their contract would allegedly be more economical at about $25,000 per year less than the cost of the existing security service.

A number of ERCOT employees had gotten to know some of the people with the existing security service company. Those exiting security guards had never heard of the new San Antonio company. Carlos was quick to point out that it was a new company composed of the best security guards from some of the much-smaller local security services. Those guards were excited to be part of a new company that was partially owned by its employees.

It didn't take long for ERCOT to experience a few minor security breaches. Some visitors were in our offices without a security badge. Some were let in without a confirmation call to their host that they had arrived. Guard positions were sometimes not manned between their shift changes. ERCOT staff began to refer to the new company as either "absent-minded security guards" or simply "absent security guards." Ken told Carlos that he had to replace those guards not doing their job.

The replacements still made mistakes. Most of them appeared to be first-time security guards. ERCOT staff stopped making fun of their incompetence and began digging into their behavior. They got to know the new guards much like they had gotten to know the previous crew. The guards were aware of their weak knowledge of procedures, blaming it on a lack of appropriate training. They shared that information with ERCOT staff.

After about four months of their ineptitude, rumors circulated about their legitimacy. More disturbing rumors emerged about possible ties to an ERCOT employee. That complaint never made it to Ken, Uranga, or Carlos. It went directly to Tom.

Tom and Margaret assigned Andrew Gallo, one of our lawyers, to investigate. The suspected employee had been identified by one of our ERCOT staff as working with Carlos. Andrew set out to confirm it.

He questioned the guard at the front desk at our headquarters. Andrew told him he had some questions pertaining to the management of their company. He showed the guard some pictures of employees who worked for Chris Uranga. They included a picture of Chris Douglas, a database manager in Uranga's group. The guard identified Chris Douglas as the chief financial officer of the new security company.

Busted!

Chris Douglas readily admitted his involvement. He, Carlos Luquis, and David Benito Cavazos, a contractor accomplice with Carlos, were arrested in an alleged conspiracy to commit fraud. Luquis and Cavazos appeared to take it in stride. They said they didn't believe that they had done anything wrong.

Chris Douglas was beside himself. He was under the impression it was all legal. He had been approached by Carlos to help out as a second job. Carlos told him that they needed some adult supervision for their clerical staff back at their main office. Carlos wouldn't have to do anything. The clerical staff took care of payroll and other disbursement details. Carlos didn't tell Chris Douglas that he had been screened by both Ken and Chris Uranga and confirmed to be unsuspecting enough to bring in. According to Chris Douglas, he had never been involved in anything like that before.

He trusted the setup that sold him on the idea that he was only doing an additional job as part of the ERCOT security contract. I felt kind of sorry for the guy. The rumor was that his wife immediately locked him out of his house and filed for divorce. He appeared to be more collateral damage than he was a a bona fide co-conspirator.

Ken and Chris Uranga were shocked. They swore off any knowledge of the fraud. Ken assured Andrew, Margaret, and Tom that he had no idea Luquis, Cavazos, and Douglas might be crooks. He didn't know that Carlos Luquis was a part-time actor. Carlos must have recruited Douglas through Cavazos to help him out as an inside contact.

Ken claimed that he was the victim, not the perpetrator. He shifted quickly into gaslighting mode. The security contract had been approved by Tom and put in place by Margaret. He assumed that they were looking out for possible fraud. Ken asked why Tom and Margaret had allowed this to happen, pointing out that they should have smelled something rotten. It was a major deflection on Ken's part to weasel out of responsibility here. But neither Tom nor Margaret ever asked me that question, about how this could happen. I could have told them how it could happen. ERCOT officers were staying in their lane.

Ken assured Tom and Margaret that he would fix the problem immediately by calling back our old security contractor.

I could never understand why Luquis didn't call out Ken. His silence supported Ken's assertion that the alleged wrongdoing had nothing to do with him. I figured that to secure any possible future support from Ken, Luquis had to be quiet.

Ken continued with business as usual. His blood bank stayed open without the security operation, of course. Ken treated the near brush with being unmasked by the security blowup as a positive. It was like he was at a blackjack table. The dealer had shown a picture card, and he had been dealt a six and a five. He presumably thrived on a game of high-risk / high reward, and now it was time to double down despite the risk. Expenditures on Steve's technology research project were getting closer to its $2 million budget. Ken stood ready to approve any needed increases to that amount.

There was no public airing of any alleged security fraud incident. It all raged on internally only. With fingers pointing in almost every direction, the officers were feeling the heat. But nobody wanted to talk about it. A new elephant entered the room yelling, "What the hell is going on here?" and sent the old "business versus technology" elephant to find work elsewhere.

The *Titanic*-like journey of ERCOT stayed the course. We had seemingly avoided the tip of a small iceberg, but the fraud event made us aware that we might be navigating through some dangerous waters. There might be some bigger icebergs on the horizon.

26
Officer Angst

Thanksgiving 2003 flew by too quickly. Thanksgiving was always my favorite holiday—a multi-day holiday with no religious overtones or gift-giving obligations. When you asked anybody what they were doing for Thanksgiving, the answer was always spending time with the family. It didn't matter who they were or where they were from, Thanksgiving was about family.

The kids flew to Austin to be with us. Sue got up at about 5 a.m. on Thanksgiving morning to prepare the turkey and put it in the oven to be ready for our family feast. She baked the best turkey with the best stuffing and the best green bean casserole and mashed potatoes. It was the only time of year for my favorite dessert—pumpkin pie. Neither Sue nor the kids liked pumpkin pie. It was all mine for the weekend. College football and a round of golf were on the agenda for my son and me. Christmas shopping on Black Friday and Saturday was the usual drill for Sue and the girls. Sunday came too soon.

As in most organizations, ERCOT's activities between Thanksgiving and Christmas were relaxed a bit. It was business as usual but with the typical holiday distractions.

The ERCOT Christmas party was held mid-December at an event center (just a big barn) outside the city limits. We rode with Rich and his wife. It was hard to find the barn in the dark, but we managed to park in its parking lot that was just a pasture.

Tom had decided to have an international theme to celebrate the diverse roots of our staff. Food stations with themed cuisine from around the world were all along the sides of the big room. It was a nice touch of class but couldn't change the mood. Everyone was thinking about the security incident.

Steve was greeting people at the entrance. He wore a tuxedo in keeping with the upscale party theme. My obsession with Ken was in high gear that night. I figured that Steve was taking everyone's temperature by the way he shook their hand and looked them in the eye. Maybe. But he was charming as always.

Ken worked the room in his usual diagnostic way. After the numerous times of seeing him talking with people, it appeared to me that each interaction was a psychiatric assessment rather than a friendly conversation. He was still in gaslighting mode. His wife couldn't make it this year. She had a commitment in Dallas. I assumed she was out of jail, but I didn't ask. "No need for a white glove dinner this year," Ken said. "Tom has it covered with this outstanding spread." He sensed the discomfort when talking with the officers. It was the new "What the hell is going on here?" elephant in the room.

I didn't see Tom smile all night. He graciously welcomed every-body. He highlighted the international theme and variety of foods. He pointed to the diversity of the staff as one of our strengths. The event wasn't about minority participation, it was about our diverse origins. It had everyone talking about their roots and fam-ilies. It was a nice icebreaker as everybody tried to avoid any urge to talk about the security incident.

Sue enjoyed the party. She loved talking with people. She could have a good conversation with a fence post. One time she was getting her nails done at a local salon. She engaged in con-versation with the girl doing her nails. She talked about our kids. Then she went on to some local news. She asked the girl about her family. The girl looked at Sue and smiled. "No speak English." Sue got a kick out of that.

The music in the background and the sound of chitchat gave me a chance to reflect on the Ken situation.

After the security incident, Ken had immediately dug into his stockpile of political capital. He was willing to use all of it if he had to. Ken was ultimately responsible for the security debacle, I'm pretty sure of it. Tom should have come down on Ken like a ton of bricks but couldn't for lack of hard evidence. Ken's huge advan-tage in political capital didn't help either.

Ken didn't give Tom the chance to raise any red flags. He stra-tegically planted seeds of suspicion about Tom and Margaret, pointing the finger at them. Why did they waive any due dili-gence review before contracting with the new security company? The security incident was their fault. In addition, he claimed, Tom, with Margaret's help, had previously hired contractors with no direct link to ERCOT's stakeholder protocols. They needed to be investigated. It was unbelievable to me that Ken's allegations actually got traction.

Not that anyone inside ERCOT really believed Tom and Margaret were guilty of any inappropriate dealings. Nor did anyone inside ERCOT really believe Tom and Margaret were mixed in with any of Ken's shenanigans. However, outside of ERCOT, particularly with local police and some stakeholders, Ken enjoyed enough success to at least confuse the issue.

ERCOT activities were split over two legal jurisdictions, and that exacerbated the problem. Our operations center in Taylor was in Williamson County. Our headquarters in Austin was in Travis County. Local officials, who had been dealing with Ken for the construction of the additional building in Taylor, stood by Ken. Local officials dealing with activity at our headquarters didn't know what to think. In fact, local officials in both jurisdictions didn't want to think. The security scam was a minor hiccup subject to a final resolution on any criminal prosecution and punishment for Luquis, Cavazos, and Douglas. Case closed—right?

Try telling that to the ERCOT officers.

I couldn't read Sam's take on the security fraud. This time, he couldn't find 100 percent comfort staying focused on "keeping the lights on." I knew it got his attention, and I was sure he was concerned, but he didn't show it. There always seemed to be a wall between Sam's operation and the rest of ERCOT. He was the most trusted officer at ERCOT—untouchable—and I think he knew it. He was always able to avoid taking sides on any controversy. I thought that this controversy might be different and that he would help Tom and confront Ken, but he didn't.

Instead, Sam let Tom squirm. As best as I could tell, he was never a fan of Tom. Four years earlier, when the board of directors brought Tom in as Sam's boss, it took a while to sort out their responsibilities. They made peace agreeing on their separate roles, their mutual strategy apparently being to stay out of each other's way as best they could. They appeared to have each other's back—usually—but not this time it seems. It was clear that regarding the alleged security fraud, Tom couldn't count on Sam to rescue him from suspicion.

Sam's relationship with Ken was difficult to read. I couldn't remember any time when they were engaged with one another in a business discussion. It appeared that Sam's relationship with Ken was about the same as his relationship with Tom. They stayed out of each other's way. I'm sure Sam was sensitive to the political capital situation that still tilted in favor of Ken. It was a situation where Sam saw no benefit to taking sides.

Maxine appeared worried, and it looked to me that she suspected there was more going on than just the security incident. I reasoned that her problem might be that she had stayed complacent too long. Perhaps she felt that her only choice was to continue to suppress her suspicions. If that were the case, it would be a tough decision, which I thought would ultimately prove to be the wrong one.

I liked Maxine. We got along really well. We had similar business training and experience as chief financial officers. I believed it was her fiduciary responsibility to fully understand what Ken was up to. She was the only one with access to the contracts and recording of disbursements. Maxine happened to be in the meeting when James asked the question, "Is that man ethical?" I knew she was worried, but the security incident still wasn't enough for her to raise a red flag about Ken. I gave her the benefit of the doubt. She might not have any hard evidence of wrongdoing.

Margaret's thinking was of the most interest to me. Her tutorial on the dismissal of any fiduciary responsibility inherent in the ERCOT quasi-governmental environment was still pretty fresh in my mind. She had stopped drinking that Kool-Aid. The security incident was a big deal. She had to know it and wound up in the middle of it only because of Ken's handiwork. I believed she was now on my side and must have realized that there was indeed a possibility that we might all eventually be fired because of Ken's schemes. Her position on the situation with Ken was the same as Maxine's: too complacent for too long. Margaret realized now that her job wasn't that easy. Just doing what stakeholders told her to do might not be enough.

Back at the office on the week after the party, Tom was a bundle of nerves. Many more than the usual number of closed-door meetings were taking place. He had years of experience dealing with company political issues, and his cool level-headed approach served him well. Conflict didn't scare him. His problem was that he was no match for Ken. He had no explanation as to why, as Ken had told everyone, neither he nor Margaret nor Maxine had caught Chris Douglas's breach of company ethics by being employed by our security contractor.

I think Ken, too, was feeling a little nervous. He wasn't getting that enthusiastic response from Margaret when talking with her. He needed some face time with his fellow officers to assess their demeanor when with him and to assure us that he was still a loyal member of our team. He arranged for Sam, Margaret, Maxine,

Ken, and me to get together for our own holiday dinner at Buca di Beppo, a homestyle Italian restaurant. Sharing entrees was his attempt to keep us feeling like family. Bonding was the intent, but Sam, Margaret, Maxine, and I were clearly keeping Ken at arm's length. Ken was upbeat and, as was his nature, tried to convince us to keep our confidence in him. He was looking forward to the new year. We had a lot of exciting things going on. He survived the security thing and couldn't hold back his relief. The rest of us struggled just to make some small talk. Any interaction we had with Ken was cool and guarded. We were preoccupied with waiting for the next shoe to drop.

The "What the hell is going on here?" elephant in the room made us all terribly uncomfortable.

27

Vacation Guilt

Sue and I had spent the previous year's New Year's Eve celebrating in Texas at a big honky-tonk in Austin. The whole country music scene was new for us. With jeans, old plain brown boots, and a collared long-sleeve shirt, I tried to blend in. We didn't know what Sue should wear. Jeans and shoes that looked almost like boots made her fit in pretty well. The women there were dressed differently. Some were straight out of a Dale Evans fashion guide. Others were dressed for a current-day night club. The music was all country. Beer was sold all around the sides of the building. We wished we had taken lessons on how to two-step. It looked like fun.

Growing up on Long Island just outside New York City, I never got into country music. It struck me as too much whining, crying, and pity partying. The songs were about people who needed to get a life. Even Elvis in the fifties seemed to me to be more like a country singer than a rock star. Dion and the Belmonts, as in Belmont Avenue in the Bronx, were much more my style.

But I loved cowboys. Western TV shows were my favorite. The list of good guys is well-known to baby boomers. Hopalong Cassidy, The Cisco Kid, the Lone Ranger and Tonto, Roy Rogers, and Annie Oakley. They could ride a galloping horse across a wide-open desert without losing their hat. I thought that was really cool. Catching bad guys in the small Western towns, each with its one classy hotel and decadent saloon, looked like fun.

It was all in my dreams living in a suburb of New York City. For my third birthday, I got a full cowboy outfit complete with boots, hat, and a holster with guns. It was captured in one of my parents' favorite pictures. I wore it while watching my favorite shows. I always wanted to go out West.

The ERCOT gig gave me the opportunity to live some of that. After finally getting settled into our house, the first clothes I bought in Austin included Western-style blue jeans, a George Strait signature shirt and two Stetson hats—one white and the other black to fit any occasion. The Hill Country of Austin certainly had that western feel. Cactus. Horses. Longhorn steers, honky-tonks, and rodeos. Shiner Bock beer and green chile stew at Chuy's Tex-Mex restaurant. I enjoyed my new environment.

But for a baby boomer like me, the real West had to be in a desert with saloons, gambling, prostitutes, and drunken men down on their luck. You know—just like Las Vegas.

Sue and I celebrated our second New Year's Eve at ERCOT with a trip to Las Vegas. We had vacationed in Vegas once or twice a year since the early eighties. We experienced its evolution from the Dunes Hotel and Casino with a nine-hole golf course to the magnificent Bellagio. I loved it. Sue seemed to really enjoy it too. The weather, the wide-open desert, the upscale resorts with lavish pools, the entertainment, gaming and free booze, the five-star restaurants—all were focused on one thing: your enjoyment, as long as you spent some time in the casino.

People-watching along the Las Vegas Strip was one of our favorite pastimes. Sue and I always looked forward to a daily walk down the Strip in the warm sunshine. We got our exercise walking from one end to the other.

I loved the Elvis impersonators. They were out there every year. Through the years they began to experience competition for photo opportunities. New characters, such as the drunken Homer Simpson, stole some attention. The nature of the Elvis impersonators evolved with an updated version of the old Elvis taking over the Strip. None of them spoke English anymore. They were happy to take a picture for a tip. After all, it was still a picture with Elvis in Las Vegas.

We did our fair share of gaming. I think Charles Fey invented the slot machine for Sue, or at least for people *like* Sue. It has a man-machine interface that is simple yet mind-boggling. The first time Sue saw a slot machine, her eyes lit up. "Hey, honey! Give me some nickels!"

The bright lights, bells, and whistles were an overstimulation for Sue. Deciding on which machine to play next was challenging. Too many options, all calling her name. Sue would play for hours but never risked a lot of money. Her volume of play was high, which was good for earning casino "comps," and her standard deviation of losses versus winnings was very low, which was good for us. At the end of the day, she would carefully count her money. She usually found a few payoff tickets that she forgot to cash. No ticket was too small—twenty-eight cents from one machine, a buck twenty from another; she would cash them in the next morning.

For me, trips to Vegas were a collection of games within a game. The big game was to win enough money at the table games to pay for the trip. We always had a head start because points from our credit card usage paid for our airfare. Casino "comps" from gaming on prior trips paid for our hotel room. Great food, a head-liner show, midnight fireworks atop the hotels along the Strip, a college football bowl games parlay, loud slots, and crowded craps tables—we earned that vacation. We enjoyed it.

The first night of this trip, Sue was at the top of her game. I caught up with her during one of my breaks from the craps tables. She was at one of her favorite penny slot machines. She put her casino players' card in the slot and pushed the $.50 button for a few spins. No winners. That machine didn't have a good feel, so she moved on to another one around the corner of the same row of machines. It was a different game but also one of her favorites.

She sat down to play and put in her money, then suddenly real-ized that she hadn't taken her casino players' card out of the slot in the previous machine. Her card was attached to an elastic strap secured to her money pouch so she wouldn't lose it. As she started to get up to retrieve it, her card came zipping around the corner, barely missing the face of a woman playing another machine. The elastic had been pulled so tight that the card popped out of the slot from the previous machine, around the corner, and back to Sue's pouch. The woman who had just narrowly escaped a major facial scarring appeared to be in shock. The elastic band must have been pulled across her machine right before she sat down.

I could only laugh as I tried to figure out the physics of how that happened. Sue apologized profusely. It was an innocent mistake and so quintessentially Sue. I liked the fun venues Vegas offered, but I realized what I really loved was being in Vegas with Sue.

The day after we arrived, I got a call from Rich. He delivered an ERCOT buzzkill. The computer system used for retail market transaction processing crashed. It was a hardware problem. Ken's problem. I said, "Well, okay, it has happened before. We have recovery processes and procedures."

Rich said, "I know, I know, but this time our friends at the Public Utility Commission want to know how you could be in Las Vegas at a time like this. Nobody knows what happened. Nobody knows when the system will be back up. And nobody knows when we will be fully recovered."

"How could nobody know what happened?" I asked. "What is Ken's staff telling us?"

"Nothing," Rich said. "Uranga has no clue. He actually seems lost. I just wanted to let you know. I'll keep you posted."

I was ticked. Here I was on vacation, having a great time with Sue, and something glitches up back at work while I am already out of town. It's not my chief area of concern, yet I'm the one getting called and put on a guilt trip. I called Ken, who said he didn't know what the problem was, but his guys were working on it. I was not surprised that he had no clue. If they had been experts in information technology maintenance and support as they should have been, Ken would already have some answers.

We didn't have a redundant operating environment for our retail market operation like we did for our "keeping the lights on" responsibility. Any analysis for adding one always failed the cost/benefit test. Now I would probably be pegged as the one who didn't demand redundant processing capabilities for the retail market process. Not to mention being on a boondoggle in Las Vegas during the outage.

I reached out to Tom to let him know my staff couldn't implement recovery procedures until Ken got the systems back up. It took almost two days to get back up and running, and then about two weeks to catch up to the normal processing of market settlements.

Most of my remaining time in Vegas was spent on the telephone with ERCOT. The two-hour time difference gave me some relief. One thing about Vegas, it's the worst place to be when a fun trip turns into a guilt trip.

28

The Shell Game

The new year would become all about investigations. The first review was initiated by ERCOT. The security incident raised concerns about our accounting and administrative internal control procedures. A review of accounting and contract administration procedures was nothing new—it was always part of our annual financial audit.

We were not currently on notice for any material problems from prior audits, so this audit had to look a little different. ERCOT requested the accounting firm to dive deeper than usual in reviewing our process of internal controls. They agreed to do so but warned us that such reviews were not targeted at fraud. That is a point that most people are surprised to hear. An accounting firm review of internal controls assumes that there are no crooks, only strengths or weaknesses in controls. I figured we had crooks, but I didn't think that digging deeper would find anything.

Internal controls cannot mitigate all exposures to fraud and abuse. Any individual internal control process ends with a manager or officer approval of a contract or cash disbursement. The internal control process always documents the dollar-limit authorizations for those managers or officers. The trust in his or her *fiduciary responsibility* is the control. It's the end of the line. If an officer is the culprit, there is no breakdown in the system of internal controls. It is fraud. The ENRON case was a perfect example. In their case, it was just a breakdown in the trust of the people at the top. More procedures wouldn't have fixed that problem, nor would they have fixed ours.

Most people are disturbed by this. They want a security blanket to guard against all possibilities of fraud and abuse. Layers upon layers of processes and procedures are often mistaken for strong controls.

This can sometimes result in a burden to employees, reducing their productivity with no gain in internal control. If you can't explain to an employee why a certain internal control process or procedure is required, then it probably isn't needed. The best internal control processes are typically limited to include only the most precise tasks whose need can be easily explained to anyone.

The review of internal controls by an outside accounting firm will identify process weaknesses. Some should be fixed, but most don't need to be. They usually fall into one of three categories: (a) excused as too costly to fix; (b) mitigated somewhere else in the process; or (c) simply immaterial.

As I expected, our accounting firm didn't find any material failure of our internal controls—because our problem wasn't about our internal controls. It was about people, not processes. It was all about fiduciary responsibility, something that Margaret was beginning to realize really should have a role in a quasi-governmental organization.

Jumping on the investigation bandwagon, Ken set up an old confidence trick, a shell game. Who might be scamming ERCOT? Tom, Margaret, or somebody else at the Taylor location? The shell game took on a life of its own. It was too bad that it got legs. But it was my opinion that it was the product of a master swindler who could confuse even the best detectives.

In my view, Ken started the game by playing the role of concerned officer. He did this by stirring up the local city fathers in Taylor. As noted earlier, Ken had made some friends in Taylor during the construction of the second building. We were visited by the closest thing to an investigator that Taylor could muster up to take a look at things. At least, that is what Ken told us.

When the investigator showed up at our facility, it appeared to me that Ken had once again tapped into an actors guild in San Antonio. This guy had to be a fellow thespian of Carlos's. I probably should have asked him if he knew Carlos, but that would tell Ken that this charade wasn't going to work.

The investigator looked like he had just walked off the set of an old John Wayne movie. He had a big hat and fuzzy eyebrows, and his eyes had an empty glare. Handlebar mustache. Suede vest with some kind of sheriff posse badge. Bolo tie. Frayed blue jeans and much too fancy cowboy boots. A big belt buckle and a purposely exposed six-shooter completed his costume. I would have never trusted this guy with a bullet.

He quietly walked around. I suppose as far as he was concerned, we were all potential perpetrators. He occasionally said hello, but acted as if he assumed he needed no introduction. Fact is, nobody knew his name. Yosemite Sam, perhaps. We didn't want to know. He was a bizarre and entertaining distraction.

His six-shooter wasn't a prop. It was real. Sam told him that we had a zero-tolerance policy for carrying a gun in the building. He would have to do any detective work without one, and that must have spooked him. Either that, or he felt like Charlie Brown's friend Linus without his security blanket. He left and never came back.

The Public Utility Commission, too, felt that they needed to do something. They couldn't let the security incident go by without their review. While it never made the newspapers, the incident was well known to our board of directors, which included the Public Utility Commission chairperson.

To their credit, the Public Utility Commission ordered a fraud investigation. They were more interested in the "who" and not just the "how" of any fraudulent activities. Unfortunately, their investigators from the state's detective pool weren't white collar crime specialists. Looking for something other than fingerprints or a murder weapon wasn't their expertise. Those investigators did the best they could but stumbled around aimlessly.

From time to time, they visited our two locations. They accumulated a chain of hearsay comments that made it look like a much more complicated setup than it was. The finger-pointing sent them in many different directions. To the amazement of many people inside ERCOT, Tom, Maxine, and Margaret were high on their list as possible accessories to some sort of scam. In my opinion, Ken had worked his shell game perfectly—he was a master of perception and deception. Tom, Maxine, and Margaret were the shells in the middle of Ken's high-stakes shell game.

The Public Utility Commission investigation sputtered. The conclusion was that we needed better internal controls. That put us right back to the review made by our accounting firm, which previously had concluded that it must be a people problem, not our internal control processes. Both the Taylor and Public Utility Commission investigations went in a big circle, 'round and 'round. That is pretty much what a crooked shell game is all about, isn't it?

The cool winter weather outside seemed to cool down the concern about the security incident. I knew it was only a small piece of something much bigger, but, as much as I wanted to, it was still too early for me to get involved. I had no hard evidence to present. My conspiracy theory wasn't any better than anybody else's. Our board of directors and the Public Utility Commission staff were still not completely satisfied. It seemed odd that the investigations came up empty. However, they had exhausted their options. ERCOT investigations were now off the table.

The "What the hell is going on here?" elephant in the room grinned from ear to ear. It knew there wasn't a pea under any of the shells. Ken had it hidden in his hand the whole time.

29

Separating the Wheat from the Chaff

Winters were fairly mild and, therefore, comfortable by day in Austin, but it could get pretty cold at night. January 2004 was no exception, although there were no ice storms this year. Walks and golf were still quite pleasant, and we looked forward to the typical Austin early spring. That's when the intense summer heat, with its occasional hailstorms and tornadoes, was still months away. We hoped that the bad weather inside ERCOT would hold off for a while as well.

Normal day-to-day stakeholder activities for the new year ramped up as usual. The transmission and distribution stakeholders and retail electric provider stakeholders worked feverishly on the retail market changes. The other stakeholder groups continued their debates on how to approach the proposed ERCOT wholesale market overhaul. ERCOT staff settled into our "Do only what you are told" routine.

It wasn't exactly business as usual for the ERCOT officers. Tom saw the writing on the wall. It looked like my group had paved the way for him to survive the retail market hot seat, but Ken's shell game was too much. Tom had announced, and the board of directors had accepted, his resignation from ERCOT effective at the end of contract period in the fall. He did his best to function as a lame duck. But we all knew he was already toast. It was pretty awkward for all of us.

I wasn't too surprised that Ken had avoided scrutiny. His political acumen was too good. Some stakeholders couldn't believe that he would even be considered a suspect. But, to my surprise, our chairman of the board made it a point to personally tell me *and* Ken that the board would be engaging an outside search firm for a new chief executive officer. That search firm would have the requisite information on our backgrounds. Apparently, some people believed that Ken was still a better pick to succeed Tom than me. Go figure.

The aftermath from the audit of internal controls and commission investigation kept Margaret and Maxine playing defense. They would assert that any breakdown in controls wouldn't happen again. The board of directors wanted to believe them but were still skeptical.

The audit and investigations had nothing to do with Sam. Sam was still "keeping the lights on." He attended the usual winter NERC meetings to get away from the ERCOT politics. The audit and investigations didn't impact me either. I stuck to my job on the retail market transformation.

Jim and Rich were firing on all cylinders, demanding clarity and precision no matter how small the task. Their managers didn't need much prodding. They enjoyed what they were doing. That had been the plan from the beginning—people working on tasks that fit perfectly with their nature. Their attitude toward their work was a combination of grinding and craftsmanship. Our staff activity to do what stakeholders told us to do and ensure their satisfaction while saving the retail market produced a near perfect business process. I'm not kidding—they were all really that good.

James found out that he had colon cancer. It was bad. He was told it was likely terminal, but he kept fighting it with meds and radiation treatment. James never blinked. He worked even harder as if the only thing on his bucket list was to complete the retail market project. My team had a single goal: to be sure they finished the project in time so that James would see the project succeed. When you saw his daily pill box with about twenty small compartments, you wanted to give him a hug. James swore he was going to beat it.

You might recall that one of Ken's lieutenants, Kevin Judice, was responsible for software applications. He was handpicked by Ken, though it wasn't clear how he got tied into him. Kevin's wife was an independent information technology recruiter. She placed a couple of technical staff in Ken's group. None of the staff hired through Kevin's wife were part of Ken's inner circle. I guessed that the prospect of lucrative placement opportunities for his wife was a factor in Kevin's decision to come work for Ken.

When Kevin came on board, he looked like another one of Ken's actors: upper thirties, athletic build, jet-black hair always combed perfectly. He had a Patrick Dempsey movie star look. I guessed he might have bypassed the San Antonio Actors Guild and come to ERCOT straight from Hollywood. I thought there was no way this guy could help us, but he did.

Kevin was the only one of Ken's lieutenants who worked well with Jim, Rich, and all of their people. He was a software tools expert as well as an expert on optimization of software application/hardware configuration environments. He let the business people tell him what application software they wanted. He would review it with them to be sure it was a good fit. He then worked with the businesspeople to optimize its performance. In short, his technology expertise complemented our business expertise. Exactly what we needed from Ken. And exactly the kind of service I expected the information technology group to provide.

Kevin seemed too honest and too capable to be one of Ken's lieutenants. He was competent and a likeable guy, and it's no wonder he interacted seamlessly with us. I had confidence in his ability. He was doing a job he loved, and it showed. I trusted him.

From time to time, Kevin would ask to meet with me just to pick my brain. He was intrigued by my experiences with software development and my engineering, CPA, and MBA background. I found out that we were on the same page when it came to "business versus technology." We talked a lot about business issues unrelated to ERCOT. Our discussions were mostly teacher/student in nature. He always thought he should have gone to graduate school. He thought it was so cool to have an in-house MBA professor. It was refreshing to have somebody at ERCOT other than Jim and Rich who appreciated my experience.

Not long after the security incident, Kevin started to raise questions with me about Ken's team. He was especially critical of Chris Uranga, whom he said had no clue as to what he was doing. He suspected Chris in the security incident but had no corroborating evidence. He was also concerned about the increase in Ken's temper tantrums directed at any staff member who was critical of Chris.

"Something is not right," said Kevin, who admitted that he felt he was being sucked into an inner circle of what appeared to be unethical behavior. He saw his being hired into Ken's group simply as a way to give Ken credibility while he (Ken), Steve, and Uranga did their thing. "I am concerned," Kevin added, "but have no one to talk to."

I got a lot of that in my career—good people asking how to get out of bad situations. Most of the time, I could tell them whom to talk to. With Kevin, I couldn't.

Like it or not, Kevin had been hired by Ken to be part of his exclusive club. If Ken were to be exposed, Kevin would automatically go down with him. I told Kevin that his best option was to resign immediately. It was easy for me to say, but hard for Kevin to do. He liked working at ERCOT, and his family was happy living in Austin.

Kevin stayed on at ERCOT, along the way keeping me informed of any new activity that seemed odd. I started to think about how I might minimize the damage to Kevin when Ken's house of cards collapsed. I was sure he had no knowledge of Ken's plans when Ken had hired him.

I also assumed he was *not* being paid by any of Ken's schemes. He wouldn't be confiding in me if he had. Kevin was either a bad guy playing me at Ken's direction or a good guy unknowingly sucked into a bad position.

I decided I would go to bat for Kevin when needed.

30

Kissing the Pig

Once a month, Tom gathered all ERCOT employees for a lunch and learn session. Free lunch, time to mingle, and information updates were the standard agenda. It was always held at an old event center in Taylor. The building was big enough to host about a thousand people—plenty big enough for our meetings of a little more than 160. It had a gray concrete floor, a kitchen area, and a couple of small restrooms. We sat at long tables to eat our buffet lunch and enjoy the festivities.

Tom wanted employees to hear what was going on in all areas of ERCOT. He was the main attraction and was always the first to give his update. Each officer then presented their update. Margaret usually shared tidbits on political and Public Utility Commission activities related to ERCOT. The Tom and Margaret presentations got the most attention. Sam, Ken, and I presented updates that most ERCOT staff pretty much knew already. The rumor mill was always busy, so the information about activities in our departments was mostly old news. At the end of our updates, Tom welcomed new staff members and asked them to stand and tell us a little bit about themselves. It was a nice touch.

After the meetings, people working for Sam, Maxine, and me would usually raise concerns about the increase of lieutenants and managers in Ken's group. Sam and Maxine didn't use Ken's group for much of anything. They hadn't increased their information technology needs since Ken came onboard. Some people in their groups were concerned about the need for so much more information technology overhead.

It always seemed to come back to the increased needs for retail market fixes and anticipated new technology needs of the expected ERCOT wholesale market overhaul project. It was accepted as true. Sam didn't really care. Tom, Margaret, and Maxine always bought into that justification.

My group didn't buy into it. Steve's project oversight position was somewhat suspicious. And there were always questions about Uranga. His qualifications didn't fit with anything related to information technology. He was spending all his time with the changes to the new physical security group. To some of us, he was already in over his head. We went along with it. We had no hard evidence to rock the boat, and we needed to work with Ken's people.

Tom also used the lunch and learns to showcase non-ERCOT business topics. Education, local events, entertainment, and fundraising were on that list. At one lunch and learn Tom was to present the results of a fundraising event conducted through an

ERCOT breast cancer research initiative. The event used an officer competition to encourage donations. The officer attracting the most donations would have to kiss a pig. The kiss would take place at a lunch and learn using a live pig.

Large glass containers were set up outside our big conference rooms at headquarters and at Taylor. Each container had the name of an officer on it. You could place money in a container as a vote for the officer you wanted to kiss a pig. Anyone could place as much money as many times as they wanted into the containers. Employees, stakeholders, or other visitors could make a contribution.

It was interesting because people were voting for a loser. That wasn't, in and of itself, all that unusual. It was intended to be like a school fundraiser where you made a contribution to throw a ball at a target to dunk a teacher. Harmless fun for a good cause.

As expected, our fundraiser evolved a little differently. It was a vote for the officer you wanted to appear a little uncomfortable in front of the entire ERCOT staff. That wasn't a bad thing for fundraising. It was a smart approach to shake loose a lot of contributions that would otherwise stick in people's pockets.

It didn't take long to see that the competition was between Ken and me. It was a popular competition. Technology versus business. The visionary versus the dinosaur. The favorite son vs. the unfavorite son, I suppose. It wasn't that spectacular, of course. But it felt like that. It was an opportunity to make a contribution to a good cause, albeit with a possible image-tainting result. It annoyed me a bit. I had enough image problems without having to add one that included kissing a pig.

The winner would be announced at the next lunch and learn. There was no doubt in my mind that Ken's staff was overstuffing my containers so that I would "win." That likelihood, along with my well-known unpopularity with the two blackballing stakeholder groups, told me that I had to be prepared to play what would be, at a minimum, the lead role in an awkward farce.

The lunch and learn for kissing the pig had the highest-ever employee attendance. The possibility of some public vetting of friction between Ken and me was hard to resist. We finished lunch and Tom set the stage for the event. The mood was festive. Margaret had dressed up like Miss Piggy to reinforce the good nature of the competition and the value of the cause. Tom thanked the women who headed the fundraiser, particularly the one who had lost her sister to breast cancer. He thanked everybody for their contributions. The fundraiser was a huge success.

The farmer and his pig sat quietly on the sideline as we enjoyed our lunch. It was a small pig. It looked like it had just jumped out of a *Three Little Pigs* book—kind of cute, but a living, snorting, snot-dripping pig, nonetheless. The poor little pig was scared shitless, literally crapping on the floor while being held by its owner. The crowd loved it. The timing couldn't have been better. It reminded all of us that, about two hours ago, this cute little thing was with its brothers and sisters playing in a pigsty. When the pig shit hit the floor, Maxine couldn't take it. She quickly left the facility.

Tom announced that I had edged above the other officers and was the winner. He invited me to step up and kiss the pig. The ERCOT staff eagerly anticipated a smart-ass remark from me. It would likely be memorable. Something offensive or something perfect for the occasion. In either case, they knew I would present it in a way that Tom wouldn't like. I still didn't have a script. My mind kept searching for a right answer.

I asked Tom if I could say a few words before consummating my relationship with the cute little sow. Like Tom, I thanked the women who headed the fundraiser. I started with the basics: "It has been quite an experience with wonderful results. My condolences to my opponents on their loss. I am honored to have attracted the highest dollar contribution."

It was time for the punchline. "Through the course of the voting, many of you anticipated I would win. I was asked how I felt about the possibility (or probability) of kissing a pig. The question I heard most often was, 'Aren't you bothered by having to kiss a pig?' My answer is pretty simple—I have been kissing asses for the last twenty-eight years, so kissing this pig is no stretch for me!"

The crowd roared with approval. I looked at Tom—he was livid. His color quickly changed from white to red to almost deep purple.

I kissed the pig. Ken didn't like me stealing the show. He stepped up behind me to kiss the pig. He posed in front of the crowd as if he was a costar in the show. For a brief moment in time, the "What the hell is going on here?" elephant had left the room. My staff was so proud of my risky one-liner. It temporarily defused tension and brought everyone together. It was a fun ending to the event.

Tom never said anything about it. But, from then on, I knew he worried about it. With Ken's shell game in play and the bug up my ass about Ken, he was quite nervous about what I might say in a public setting.

Whether it was in a public setting or in private, I had to make my point my way. I never minced words. He knew that too. Tom was right to be worried.

31
Matthew 4:8-10

Again, the devil took Him to a very high mountain and showed Him all the kingdoms of the world and their glory; and he said to Him, "All these things I will give You, if You fall down and worship me." Then Jesus said to him, "Go, Satan! For it is written, 'you shall worship the Lord your God, and serve him only.'

—Matthew 4:8-10

I was raised in the Catholic faith. At 10 years old, it seemed strange to me that I had to go to church every week when my parents never went. They dropped me off and then picked me up on time at the designated location away from the church traffic. It was hard to understand. I assumed it was one of those benefits you got when you became an adult.

I had a Mass missal that I took to church every Sunday, but the Bible was our ultimate religious reference book. Our family had a very large copy with gold-trimmed pages, colorful cloth bookmarks, and a bright red leather cover.

I never read it. Probably because it was never required reading. I never read anything unless it was required reading. I did flip through the pages one time in search of the Adam and Eve chapter. One of my friends had told me that some Bibles had great naked pictures of Eve. Sure enough. We had one.

Reading never agreed with me. It always put me to sleep. Every Sunday, I opened my missal to the right page for that day's Mass. The small print was too hard to read, and I had no idea what the priest was saying in Latin. I looked forward to the gospel readings. They were in English. It was a lot easier to listen to gospel readings at church rather than fumble through the missal. I did retain a fair amount of gospel content.

Nuns at church school were scary strict. Easily stereotyped, never smiling. I sort of understood that. Trying to teach religion to a class full of 10-year-old kids who didn't want to be there couldn't have been fun. Then again, God's work wasn't all fun. They were really good people doing really good things for very little compensation other than spiritual satisfaction.

I was told about all the fringe benefits I would earn by going to Catechism class after a hard day at school. The promise of a one-way ticket to heaven was enticing, but it wasn't enough. I just didn't like it. There had to be an alternative route to heaven. The only thing worse than Thursday afternoon Catechism class was the cold bus ride from the church back to my school. I was always afraid of walking home in the dark.

Catechism teaching during my formative years was based on guilt and fear. The notion of black marks on my soul—small ones for venial sins, large black splotches for mortal sins—scared the shit out of me. The buildup of guilt was intense. It was hard to put into perspective.

That whole Catholic approach changed over time. There were still some remnants of fear and guilt teachings when my kids attended their Catechism classes years later, but it never seemed to faze my oldest daughter. She took it all in stride from the get-go.

Sue went with her to her first confession and proudly watched her enter the confessional. After a few minutes, a roar of laughter could be heard coming from the priest's booth. When our daughter came out, Sue asked what that was all about. My daughter said, "Well, I went through my list, and I stopped to think if I got it all. The priest asked me, 'Is that all you want to tell me, my child?' I told him, 'There are a few other small things, but there is a really long line out there, and we should move along so you can hear from all of them.'" She was so much like her mother.

Things are different now. I'm so glad that the Catholic church made so many changes to make it better. It is now a source of strength and peace rather than guilt and fear. For me, it has been quite a transformation.

Apparently, ERCOT was also about to go through a transformation. I didn't know it. My peers didn't know it. Our board of directors didn't know it. But it appeared that Ken and Steve did.

With the prospect of escalating suspicion and increasing complexity of covering their tracks, Ken and Steve were finally showing signs of feeling some heat. It was unlike them to show any sign of such concern. Without even a hint as to why, their usual mostly jolly and mischievous moods turned serious. Something had gone wrong. Their situation had changed. They had to make a move.

Whatever had happened, Ken couldn't sweep it into a cloud of Keystone Kop-like confusion. It required help from someone outside their inner circle. The profile they developed was so typical of Ken and Steve. They needed someone with unimpeachable credibility to fortify any effort that might be needed to defend their activity. I had no hard evidence, but it was suddenly crystal clear to me that they were stealing from ERCOT. Somebody had connected the dots.

They needed somebody with unquestionable honesty and integrity, just like it said on the pyramids Ken had given out at his white glove dinner a year or so earlier. It had to be someone they could prop up as king, but who would still owe them for getting him the crown. It had to be someone who wanted it more than anything and was willing to sell out to them to get it.

They had made a calculated play. Steve called me and said that he and Ken wanted me to succeed Tom as chief executive officer. He said that ERCOT had a leadership void that needed to be filled sooner rather than later. With my management acumen and their political capital, we could get things back on track. There was no need for ERCOT to look outside for a new chief executive officer.

Ken and Steve were so knowledgeable of the human condition and so diabolical in their use of that knowledge. It was almost a religious experience. They reached into my very soul with the promise of the respect and stature I craved deep inside. For me, it was one of those significant emotional events that sticks with you the rest of your life.

To be brutally honest, I did feel that my career would end in underachievement without a final tour of duty as a chief executive officer. I felt like the training, hard work, and results were all there to warrant serious consideration somewhere, even if it was not at ERCOT.

For a split second, I actually considered it. I believed that they had the political capital to do it. Take the job and fire them all. Of course, that was absurd. For some reason, one of my favorite gospel readings immediately came to mind. It was Matthew 4:8-10.

> Again, the devil took Him to a very high mountain and showed Him all the kingdoms of the world and their glory; and he said to Him, "All these things I will give You, if You fall down and worship me." Then Jesus said to him, "Go, Satan! For it is written, 'you shall worship the Lord your God, and serve him only.'

I knew that the only way I would take on a chief executive officer promotion would be if it came as a result of serious consideration of our board of directors through their standard process. It couldn't come from part of a scheme cooked up by two con men such as Ken and Steve. Like Judas, I wouldn't be able to live with myself if I even considered their offer.

My answer was easy, but it needed to be respectful enough to avoid an all-out assassination attempt on me from them. I told Steve, "Thanks, but no thanks. If I am to be chief executive officer, it has to happen organically through the board of directors' process."

That episode was surreal—another one of those things that only happens in the movies. What happened next was even more unbelievable.

32

Dead Man Walking

Afternoons during the summer in Austin can be brutal. It was hot outside. I don't know how construction workers on rooftops survived. They were smart enough to put more clothes on to avoid burning to a crisp. I admired the street smarts and work ethic of those who pushed their bodies to the limit every day to support their families. It was a daily reminder to keep things in perspective.

Air conditioners kept it cool inside. Sam told the board of directors, "We hit another summer peak in electricity usage." This was prime time for Sam and his staff: Attention to detail. Everything by the book. No hiccups in electricity service due to ERCOT error.

Jim and Rich did their thing. No hiccups on our end either.

I waited patiently for something big related to Ken and Steve. Jim and Rich hadn't heard anything new about them from their staff. I shared my religious experience with Jim and Rich. I told them that Steve and Ken wanted me to be the new chief executive officer. To say they were surprised would be an understatement.

After they got over their shock, we talked about what might come next. Perhaps Ken and Steve had a traitor in their midst. It was an eerie feeling of anticipation.

The "What the hell is going on here?" elephant in the room had become the virtual chairperson of the board of directors. Board members were still trying to understand what the hell was going on. Their hope was that the security incident was the only thing wrong. A single rogue contractor. The board wasn't comfortable simply hoping. The financial audit gave them no answers, and they wanted to know the breadth and depth of what was going on. That included the uncomfortable continued discussions about the possible involvement of Tom, Margaret, and Maxine.

They created a special investigation committee. Miguel Espinoza chaired the committee. Miguel was one of four unaffiliated board members with no previous direct ties to ERCOT. Sixty-seven and retired, he was a highly respected well-known businessman from Houston. Miguel had thirty-five years of experience at one of the big oil companies. He was a finance guy serving as treasurer in his final years of work. Politically talented and plugged in, he had been a college roommate of a future U.S. senator and was a no-nonsense guy who had seen just about everything in the oil business.

The special investigation committee was to sort out the suspected problems that spawned the extra efforts of the financial audit, Public Utility Commission investigation, and investigations by local officials. Auditors and local investigators had been tangled up in the web woven by Ken and his cohorts. The loose ends were too significant to ignore. They needed to be cleaned up.

It was no surprise that the actions of Tom, Maxine, and Margaret were still under scrutiny. Ken's shell game had worked to perfection. They couldn't go on the offensive as long as they were part of the problem and not included as part of the solution. They had to play defense as best they could. The harder they played defense, however, the more anxious and suspicious they appeared. They couldn't ignore it. To do so would also be interpreted as an attempt to avoid suspicion.

Employees hesitated to go to them with information for fear of being sucked into suspicion. Everybody hated the tension, but nobody would do anything about it. Even if anybody had any hard evidence, they didn't have the risk-preferred profile to come forward. There was no winning attached to voicing a concern. Too bad that they weren't employees owning some stock in a "for-profit" ERCOT. With a portion of their nest egg at risk, they might have felt differently.

Ken and Steve continued their gaslighting to continue to confuse anyone drilling down on the security incident. It was working much too well for them. But there was that uneasiness that they seemed be dealing with when they had called me about the offer to be chief executive officer. A piece of their angle must have developed a sharp edge that Ken and his conspirators couldn't grind down. There must have been some sort of breakdown in their ranks—a leak perhaps. Or better yet, a misstep that might bring them down with a total exposure of their dishonesty.

Less than a month after the call to me from Steve, he resigned, citing medical conditions that would keep him on pain medication and out of work. It got me to wondering if perhaps Steve had had any sort of affinity for pain medications beyond what they had been prescribed for, as this was about the time that media reports of growing cases of addiction to pain medicine were generating headlines. I had no evidence to suggest Steve had a problem in this regard, for if he did, that sort of thing surely would have come up in a background check—a background check that Gary Stroud was never able to complete.

Steve might have found out what was coming before he resigned. It was a game changer. The shit hit the fan when the front-page headline in a Dallas Sunday newspaper read:

"Why Did ERCOT Pay a Dead Man?"

33

Truth, Integrity, Trust, and Honor... Part II

The name Chip Weeden immediately came to mind. He was the lawyer who had resigned from Margaret's staff. I had expected he might have had good reason to resign. I didn't know for sure, but I believed he had tipped the newspaper about the Ken and Steve shenanigans. The investigative reporters had to be pretty well informed by an ERCOT insider. They knew the name of the dead man. He had to be linked to an ERCOT contract by one of our employees. Somebody at ERCOT had to have called the newspaper to put them on the right track. Chip was at the top of my list. We never found out who did it. But Chip had my vote as the ERCOT "Deep Throat."

The investigative reporters for that story did a superb job with their research. What stuck out in their piece was how Steve had botched his part in the con job. Under contracts Ken had set up, Steve authorized payments to the brother of an old high school friend. I guess Steve thought he could pay off his old friend if needed. Steve didn't know that the brother of his old high school friend had been dead for more than a year before the scheduled phony payment to him. In addition, the story revealed that Steve was still on probation for a 1999 conviction for attempting to procure prescription painkillers.

Poor Gary Stroud. Our human resources guy that never got a chance to do a background check on Steve also never got a chance to defend himself. He was fired immediately. He never took another job as a human resources manager and probably would never have gotten one anyway. He took a teaching assignment at a local community college. The reduced stress of an academic environment was more to his liking. He said that he could live with the trade-off of less stress for lower pay. I don't think he believed it. It was sad to see a man lose his spirit due to the dishonesty and incompetence of others.

It was also sad to see the best investigative work emerge from news reporters instead of the ongoing audits and law enforcement initiatives. There was no questioning the truth in the report. The evidence had been confirmed. There were no embellishments, just the facts. I was happy to finally see a meaningful probe with a focus on people rather than process. Breaking the news in the Sunday morning headline probably sold a lot of papers, but was a bit of a low blow to Tom and our board of directors. There was no prior notice to anyone at ERCOT as to what was to be published.

Tom broke the news to the board of directors. Of course, it wasn't news for them. They had all read the Sunday paper. The headline sparked a Texas firestorm. It was the last straw. The board of directors thanked Tom for his service. They thought it best for him to leave now instead of on his contract ending date in the fall.

Tom had been trying to obtain a contract renewal for two more years. There would be no more discussions about a possible additional term. That was it for Tom.

Ken, a former lead candidate to succeed Tom, stuck to his script. He denied any wrongdoing and continued to point fingers at others. There was no question that Tom, Margaret, and Maxine were in deeper shit now. But Ken wasn't going to be exonerated by claims of others' wrongdoing. He had brought Steve in based on his own representation of Steve's stellar qualifications. Ken was probably beside himself about Steve's fumble, but nobody could tell. We never saw him after the newspaper headline. Ken and Uranga were immediately placed on leave of absence until further notice.

Ken's stories from the first day we met came to mind: His wife being detained in jail on questionable real estate fraud charges. A wife I still hadn't met. And the eeriest story from that first day was Ken's prediction. He said that he was here to make ERCOT's information technology operation noteworthy for Sunday morning newspaper headlines. And, within about eighteen months, he did just that.

Sam was named acting chief executive officer. For once, I knew he was happy that I was on board. He had only half of ERCOT's operations to worry about, and that half was his that ran itself pretty well already. He was able to temporarily take on additional administrative duties without too much extra effort. Even though they were simply staying in their lanes, Margaret and Maxine were tainted, but still in control of their activities. For the next few months, before the board of directors brought in an outsider as chief executive officer, the four of us worked really well together.

The collateral damage of the news report of ERCOT paying a dead man was tough on all ERCOT employees. Their friends and neighbors knew they worked at ERCOT. They were all sullied by the public airing of ERCOT's dirty laundry.

Working for ERCOT was no longer a prestigious job. Our once-proud ERCOT team, hard at work doing something new and exciting in the old sleepy electric utility business, now had to lay low. Even walking the dog was sometimes difficult: "Hey, Mary, you work for that ERCOT outfit, don't you? What the hell is going on over there?" There was something about fraud in a quasi-governmental entity funded by the public. It hit home with our neighbors much more than fraud in a private corporation that hurt only private investors.

About thirty pyramids engraved with "Truth, Integrity, Trust, and Honor" were thrown across the front yard of Ken's house. His former disciples were really pissed.

34

Hard Evidence

It wasn't long after being placed on leave of absence that Ken and Uranga were fired. The whole "Why did ERCOT pay a dead man" thing had a domino effect as expected. Anything related to Ken was thrown under the bus. My colleague, Kevin, found himself in hot water. He had been named Ken's interim replacement but was in our lawyers' crosshairs. Kevin had been hired by Ken and was assumed to be a conspirator.

I wanted to help Kevin. His only guilt was through his association with Ken. I went to bat for him. I talked with Andrew Gallo. We agreed that it would be best for Kevin to resign. We also agreed that he would remain fair game should there be any evidence to tie him to any stolen money.

Kevin was devastated but knew that was the right thing to do. No money was ever traced to Kevin. In fact, there was never a need to call him in for further questioning. He survived the ordeal and would sustain a successful career in huge transaction-based software applications.

Kevin's need to confide in me was soon to be outdone. Another ERCOT employee, Mike Petterson, our accounting manager, called me for a confidential conversation. "I am concerned but have no one to talk to."

Déjà vu all over again. Another good person asking how to get out of a bad situation. The public display of probable scandal put a lot of people at ERCOT in a bad situation. I was curious that this was coming from Mike and not his boss, Maxine.

Mike was an endurance bicycle rider. An Austin resident, Lance Armstrong, was his idol. Mike rode in the early morning before work and again after work well into dusk. His face was highlighted with high cheekbones and sunken cheeks. He had zero body fat, or pretty close to it, and he always looked like he was ready for the start of a triathlon—alert and good to go.

We weren't close friends, but I believed I knew him well enough to trust him. He was about to place a lot of trust in me. He had connected some dots but wasn't sure what to do with it. He wanted me to look at some hard evidence and to get my thoughts.

Hard evidence was something that nobody, other than the newspaper reporters, seemed to have. If any was to surface, it would have to come from Maxine or Margaret or both. I had pretty much given up hope on seeing that. Their adherence to the quasi-governmental standard of working with blinders on meant there was very little chance that we would ever see any hard evidence. They had gotten caught in Ken's web. Maybe Mike's contact with me was the only way for them to get out.

Mike laid it out for me. Shortly after Steve set up the technology research project, there were fixed monthly obligations set up for certain contracts authorized by Ken with individual contractors authorized from time to time by Steve to perform the work. Margaret put those contracts together under pressure from Ken and Steve. I guessed that she was told that these were mission critical contracts that we would lose if not signed quickly. Given the urgent request and her belief that she need only stay in her lane, she didn't pay any attention to the business content. That was solely Steve and Ken's responsibility. From Margaret's standpoint, her job was limited to a legal review, not as a fiduciary. The contracts were clearly legally binding.

Two of them really stuck out. The monthly fixed-payment amounts for the two contracts, $50,000 and $75,000, were routinely authorized by Ken. Mike's boss, Maxine, set up the payments as specified in the contracts. From Maxine's standpoint, the amounts were properly accounted for and properly paid. She, too, opted to stay in her lane, never asking about deliverables. Execution and quality of deliverables was Steve's problem, not hers.

In the overall quasi-governmental scheme of things, everyone was simply doing their job.

The front-page headline about paying a dead man had raised everybody's awareness. Mike told me he thought he had hard evidence that Ken had the pea to his shell game in his hand during his entire implementation of that ruse. He was playing a devilish game using Tom, Maxine, and Margaret as shells. That really wasn't news to me, but then he asked, "Ray, would you take a look at what I have?"

Mike didn't say it, but my gut feeling was that both Margaret and Maxine advised Mike to come to me. They were both already in a weakened position. Both had trusted the process and stayed in their lanes. As a result, they had given their tacit approval of those contracts. It is a fiduciary responsibility fear that makes somebody like me a pain in the ass. Quasi-governmental or not, contracts have to make business sense. Tacit approval instead of explicit approval is no escape.

To run with the hard evidence, Margaret and Maxine needed to give the information either to Sam or to me. I didn't think they would go to Sam. He was much too busy "keeping the lights on." He would likely defer any dealing with administrative problems under his temporary status as interim chief executive officer to Tom's permanent replacement, whenever he arrived. Besides that, Sam was a stay-in-your-lane believer like Maxine and Margaret. He might see Ken's wrongdoing as an unfortunate consequence of the quasi-governmental environment. From his standpoint, it might be best to leave it alone. There was no significant harm, no action-worthy foul. So ERCOT loses some money. So what? No reason for anyone else to get hurt. Steve was already gone. Ken and Uranga were already gone. Why stir up more controversy?

Margaret and Maxine really had only one choice. They had to come to me. I was the in-house fiduciary responsibility fanatic. They knew that I had been on Ken's case from the day we both came onboard. They assumed that I already had a whole lot of hearsay reference points. They also assumed I had the stomach for the risk associated with putting it all out there.

I wasn't sure that all of those assumptions were true, but Mike came to me for whatever reason. He gave me a copy of a printout of the accounting records for fixed monthly payments. He also gave me a copy of the contracts.

For the first time since joining ERCOT, I thought about the merits of staying in my lane. Is it worth being in the know, or not? As Sam might say, "What's the point of stirring up more controversy? This could blow up in your face. It could be a premature end to your career. All that you worked for would go down the drain. Think of Sue and the future. Your nest egg vs. ethics. Why risk it simply because you want to do what is right?"

The answer was clear. I'm a fiduciary responsibility junkie and passionate about punishing bad guys, especially those who prey on the trust of other people. It's my nature. It's my thing. This is what I do. Think of all the good people here at ERCOT that need this fraud to be totally exposed. Think of how much bigger this problem could have gotten if Ken had had an opportunity to take his production nationwide. There is no downside to doing the right thing. Sue would be so disappointed if I chose to bury my head in the sand. It was time to apply my expertise to set the record straight.

I didn't have to dig too far into my fiduciary responsibility bag of corporate no-no's. The fraud was immediately obvious to me. The statement of work in those contracts called for no deliverables, no minimum hours, no final report. The contracts required nothing but monthly payments from ERCOT to the contractor—early a scam as defined in any dictionary!

How could we enter into contracts with fixed monthly payments and no delivery obligations? The answer was a no-brainer. It's all quasi-governmental, remember? It's easy. Everybody doing their job, and only their job, as approved by stakeholders. No complicated officer fiduciary responsibilities to shareholders; just do what you are told to do by stakeholders.

Then hope that investigative reporters don't get a lead. If they do, don't count on those stakeholders to bail you out.

35
Stepping Up

There were no pregnant pauses around ERCOT's water coolers. ERCOT staff had plenty to talk about. What do we tell the stakeholders? Was anyone other than Steve involved? Who tipped the newspaper reporters? Would Ken and Uranga go to jail? Was anyone else involved? Would anyone else be fired? How will ERCOT be punished? Will trauma counseling be available to us? Who will be our new chief executive officer? Okay, the trauma counseling question was bad a joke. But our uncertain future wasn't funny.

We couldn't bury our collective heads in the sand and wait for the storm to blow over. New investigations by local officials were proposed. Here we go again—more fumbling and bungling of local law enforcement. Surely, more than that would be done.

Ken and Steve didn't wait to see where it might go. They lawyered up. Their lawyers did what lawyers do best—muddy the waters. They did a better job than Ken and Steve had been doing by themselves. Their defense of no wrongdoing was holding up surprisingly well.

I had heard that Steve explained away his mistake as a senior moment even though he wasn't quite old enough for that. That brother of his former classmate had done some work for him before. Of course, nobody would buy into any representation that it was a simple paperwork error.

Ken pointed to the legal nature of everything he did, proclaiming that he had trusted Steve, and, besides, this is just something that officers do. He continued by insisting that even if what he delivered wasn't liked, it was all legal and above board. He also verbally brought Tom, Margaret, and Maxine into his court by claiming they knew exactly what he had been doing.

It came back full circle again to Tom, Margaret, and Maxine. They were taking bigger hits from Ken and Steve's lawyers than those thrown their way after the security incident. For them, it could now involve more than simply being fired.

They were never formally accused of any wrongdoing. They didn't lawyer up. They still considered it solely an ERCOT thing. They knew they didn't do anything wrong. They stayed in their lane. It was not a personal legal matter. That is what they hoped would continue to be the case. Of course, there are no corporation safeguards to defend against personal liability in a quasi-governmental entity. It's every man and woman for himself/herself in these situations.

The investigative committee of the board of directors, the Public Utility Commissioners and staff, and legislators pulled the plug on investigations by local officials. They finally hit on the right answer: They had a duty to preserve the public trust in ERCOT. It was good to see that somebody finally realized they had some kind of duty to uphold within the quasi-governmental environment. Even if it proved to be only a tempest in a teapot, the Texas state attorney general, Greg Abbott, had to be brought in.

The biggest problem for the attorney general's office was the nature of any possible crimes. They included the security incident in their scope, which still only showed the unacceptable related party agreement with Chris Douglas. That was pretty weak evidence of wrongdoing. Luquis, Cavazos, and Douglas were already accused and free on bail. Other than Douglas being an ERCOT employee, their crime wasn't clear. There was no hard evidence to tie them to any conspiracy. In addition, except for Steve's alleged senior moment, accusations against Ken, Steve, and Uranga were only hearsay. And any involvement of Tom, Margaret, or Maxine had to be considered. Compounding the problem was that Texas had no white-collar crime unit. It didn't matter. The attorney general's office pushed ahead and took dead aim at the "What the hell is going on here?" elephant in the room.

Abbott immediately considered a grand jury investigation. He would have to put a case together the best he could. Names and hard evidence had to exist somewhere in this mess. They needed to find them and explain how they fit into a conspiracy to defraud ERCOT.

It was all coming together. I wouldn't have too much time to think about what to do with my newfound hard evidence. The answer came right to my doorstep the day after I received the information from Mike Pettersen.

That afternoon, all of the ERCOT managers, plus me, were asked to attend a meeting with a prosecutor from Greg Abbott's office. We sat around a large table in one of our big conference rooms. Sam, Margaret, and Maxine were not present. They would be interrogated individually. There was an unsettling quiet in the room. Everyone stared at one another inquisitively. What was this all about? Why did we have to meet with someone from the attorney general's office?

It was new territory for the bright young attorney, David Glickler, assigned by the attorney general to the ERCOT case. He was a plain-talking Texan with a polished demeanor of a state senator. I would later find out that his easygoing manner was merely part of his total package. He was a pit bull-like prosecutor. My colleagues expected David Glickler to lead with his pit bull side. Instead, he chose to build trust with us through a casual and friendly approach. His message was clearly that of an exasperated prosecutor. With a calm but stern voice, he wanted to know, "What the hell is really going on here?"

David couldn't bang down any doors or issue a summons for any confidential financial records without a good reason. He knew that we knew stuff. Hearsay or anonymous tips wouldn't cut it. He wanted evidence, preferably hard evidence. His plea was both respectful and intimidating. He knew it was a high-risk, no-reward proposition for anyone stepping up. It was unlikely he would find anyone in a quasi-governmental organization to take such a risk. He really didn't expect a response but had to ask for help. He pointed to our duty to preserve the public trust in ERCOT. This was about sending the conspirators to jail; it was about the reputation of ERCOT.

David's appeal to our duty to ERCOT was taken as an option to stick your neck out for no compensation and not a compelling legal responsibility. His plea of "What the hell is really going on here?" was a bit intimidating. But it was also disappointing.

It told all of us that the attorney general's office didn't know anything new. They knew what we knew and that was it. A circumstantial case for conspiracy could be made, but it would be weak. David would have to address the roles of Tom, Margaret, and Maxine. To anybody outside the quasi-governmental world of "staying in your lane," they were hardly innocent bystanders. It also told us that the attorney general's office had no hard evidence of fraud.

Almost everyone in the room came to the same conclusion. Don't get involved. This too shall pass. I couldn't blame them. Anything new that they might have to share was probably the result of third-party gossip. There were no new clear facts. The "What the hell is going on here?" elephant in the room ran away in fear. It wasn't an amusing diversion anymore. It was now some serious shit.

It was finally the right time and the right place for me to step up. David was the first law-enforcement person I met who could understand how the pieces fit together. He was the person I had been waiting for with whom to share my story. He would get it. I raised my hand and spoke confidently to David. "I'll tell you precisely what's been going on. I'd like to share with you how I think everyone and every circumstance fits perfectly into a complete picture." He pointed at me and smiled. "I want to talk to you in private. Anybody else?"

Was he kidding? My colleagues couldn't get out of the room fast enough. Again, I couldn't blame them. It was some serious shit.

36

"Opportunity"—
A Classified Chef d'oeuvre

Decorations for Halloween were everywhere. Ghosts, ghouls, witches on broomsticks, and bats. The bats were real. There were bats in caves in the hills. Bats in the sides of buildings.

Most notably in downtown Austin, there were bats under the South Congress Bridge. About a million and a half of them. They regularly flew out from under the bridge about twenty minutes before sundown. It was a tourist attraction. Sue and I went down to see them. We had to play tourist for that attraction at least one time. That was enough. It might have been an off day for them. They flew too low and made an odd screeching sound. Portrayals of bats give them too much love. In real life, they are scary, nasty creatures.

The bats under the bridge were Mexican free-tailed bats. They kept the insect population down. Insects were a gourmet meal for them. Large amounts of droppings from those bats were once a popular source of natural fertilizer. I'd hate to see that disclosure these days on the side of a can of string beans.

They are not to be confused with vampire bats who feast on birds. The approach of vampire bats is to cut a slit in the bird and lick its blood. Of course, vampire bats are not to be confused with vampires that suck blood directly out of people. The good news was that the vampires preying on ERCOT were about to become extinct.

I was about to get my fifteen minutes of fame. It was to take place in a closed-door, confidential grand jury hearing room. Since the proceedings were strictly confidential, there wasn't really any fame to go with it. I figured that my short visit would be as close as I'd ever get to any kind of fame, so I approached it that way to reassure myself this was the right thing to do. There had to be some benefit to me to testify. After all, if I said something wrong, I could go to jail.

I wasn't nervous, but, being prone to worry a lot, I anxiously anticipated the event. The facts that I had agreed to share had been falling into place almost every day over the past two years. It had been hard to ignore the false impressions Ken and Steve had been painting of me, Tom, Margaret, Maxine, and others who got in their way from time to time. Their misleading artistry had no regard for the hurt it might cause. What I really looked forward to was finally getting to paint a picture portraying my view of the debacle. It would include not only the diabolical reality of their scheme, but also the injustice they caused for so many good people.

Prior to the hearing, I sketched it out for David. I was to paint a complete picture that would leave no misunderstanding of what happened. The theme of my version of a twenty-first-century realism masterpiece was "Opportunity." It would communicate how it happened, but, more importantly, why it happened.

The background setting of my painting had to bring our audience into the ERCOT environment to make it much easier for them to understand why it had happened. They had to first see the canyon-sized opportunities enabled by the ERCOT quasi-governmental structure. They had to feel the false sense of comfort brought on by ERCOT employees working with blinders on and simply doing only what stakeholders told them to do.

Further details would be shared to show how the trappings of the "no limits" Stakeholders' Golden Rule fit so well with the quasi-governmental background. The elements of The Stakeholders' Golden Rule were an important transitional part of the picture. The Stakeholders' Golden Rule created the environment of limitless spending to attain the greater good. By its nature, it required that there be no controls. Project plans didn't need clear deliverables or firm deadlines. Project overruns were rewarded with additional funding instead of disciplining consequences. By looking at those trappings, you would be able to understand why the fraud could happen and begin to see how it happened.

The very rules of the game at ERCOT created limitless opportunity for well-intentioned but unnecessary spending at best, and/or fraudulent activities at worst. Our audience would have to have that clear background picture of the *opportunity* that facilitated the bad behavior.

So, what about the painting in the foreground? That had to address the questions in the minds of the jurors. The biggest question would likely be, "Who are the 'good guys' and who are the 'bad guys'?" Our painting had to make that distinction crystal clear. The jurors were new to the case. I had to assume that, as far as they could tell, everybody looked like they had a role in the craziness. They still saw it all as a shell game.

My painting had to give them the clear picture: Tom, Maxine, and Margaret were the "good guys" at the mercy of Ken and Steve, who were the "bad guys." That had to be the primary takeaway for observers of my painting. No more shell games. No more confusion.

The "good guys" didn't determine *why* money needed to be spent for any given project. The "bad guys" did. The "good guys" didn't determine *how much* money needed to be spent. The "bad guys" did. The "good guys" didn't determine *when* the money needed to be spent. The "bad guys" did. The "good guys" didn't determine *who got paid*. The "bad guys" did. By his actions, it was evident that Ken saw that taking advantage of the opportunities at ERCOT was easier than shooting fish in a barrel. All he needed was the right people; the processes were already in place.

The "good guys" believed that the "bad guys" were adhering to their responsibility to act, as dictated by the stakeholders and stakeholder protocols . . . all to achieve the greater good. It was the responsibility of the "bad guys" to live up to any obligation to preserve the public's trust in government.

Jurors might be wondering why all the investigations came up with no answers. They would need to understand that the investigations were always focused on the activities of the "good guys."

Procedures followed by auditors only involved the internal controls that had been established to check the activities of "good guys." In addition, investigators were always encouraged by the "bad guys" to investigate the "good guys." That is what they did. The result was a mess. Only the "good guys" got investigated and audited. Nobody audited or investigated the activities of the "bad guys." That is what got us here.

That would be enough painting to set the stage. I would then get to the main characters and their confidence game. I would paint Ken and his lieutenants as part of the new breed of expert, twenty-first-century con men: Politically astute and charming. Technology savvy enough to appear credible when called upon to perform. If you looked only at their acting prowess, it was hard to believe that they were the "bad guys." But underneath the smooth exteriors were their greed and willingness to deceive in any way needed to get what they wanted.

I told David that the centerpiece of my painting would have the attention to detail needed to complete a picture for indictment. The jurors would not be able to see it any other way. The hard evidence would leave no doubt about the scam. It would be irresponsible to let these guys get away without a deep dive into their personal financial activities.

It all fit. David couldn't wait to put me on the stand.

37
Justice and Exoneration

I arrived early to the hearing room and sat in a side chair in the jury chamber. One of the jurors came in and told me I was not allowed in the jury room until called. Another one of my meaningless but highly embarrassing blunders. David came in and apologized to the juror. He assured him I wasn't familiar with the process, just excited to be there. He took me into the side chamber.

David went to the jury room to prepare my canvas—not exactly the Sistine Chapel, but still the most appropriate place for my masterpiece. I wasn't anxious anymore. I was now nervous but in a good way. I made one final check to be sure my color palette and brush were ready to paint my masterpiece. One more deep breath.

I knew there would be no payment for my work. Not even any kudos from teachers and students of fine art. Nobody would see my masterpiece. It would remain under lock and key.

I don't know if anybody else testified before the grand jury. I do know that that David Glickler was quite pleased with my masterpiece.

The post-grand jury investigation was different than all the other confused detective explorations. The suspects were clearly identified. The hard evidence provided grounds for search warrants.

Uranga was now on his own. He couldn't afford a lawyer and was the first to crack. Douglas was in the same boat as Uranga. He would tell anybody anything they wanted to know. His role in the security part of the scam gave David some insights into the entire operation. Luquis and Cavazos, the other security scammers, never did come clean. They maintained that they were just doing their jobs.

It was satisfying to see Greg Abbott's news conference on television announcing the indictment of the "ERCOT rogue employees." He had a chart with their pictures and lines drawn between them like a diagram of a Mafia family operation. Perhaps a bit too melodramatic, but an effective communication, nonetheless. It included the security scammers who finally admitted that they had been working for Ken.

David still had to get convictions. The security scammers and Uranga entered pleas, but Ken and Steve were the big fish to catch. Their lawyers continued to make things difficult.

Search warrants were highest on David's to-do list. The two ERCOT contracts and paying a dead guy were enough probable cause. David filed the detailed description of places to be searched.

He didn't bother with things in plain view such as Steve's house or Ken's Mercedes. He didn't go after any of their travel information either. The "absence of evidence of possibly legitimate income" was not a path David wanted to pursue. It would take too much time and would be too complicated a case that might veer too far off track.

David knew that Ken's and Steve's financial records were the key to finding the money trail needed to quickly and effectively secure convictions. He obtained search warrants for their bank accounts and any related bank accounts. The objective was to get convictions that would stick as fast as possible and, through restitution, to get back as much money as possible.

Ken and Steve had set up a somewhat complicated maze of bank accounts that took some time for investigators to sort through. Bank transfers were always made in small-enough amounts to avoid suspicion. But there was no avoiding the deposits from the two contracts for monthly payments of $50,000 and $75,000 from ERCOT. They were identified and traced through to the accused. Unfortunately for Ken and Steve, there was no avoiding that low-hanging fruit. Those contracts accounted for most of the amount recovered by ERCOT in restitution.

The arrest of Ken was uneventful. It must not have been his first rodeo. Apparently, he took it in stride. I wasn't surprised that his wife was out of town on business and missed the festivities.

Steve's arrest was much more dramatic. As you might expect, he was allegedly very sick and had to be dragged away from a crying wife and other family members and friends. You could always count on Steve to put on a pretty good show. It was sad but a fate he clearly earned.

None of the conspirators ever went to trial. Pleas were made, resulting in some jail time and restitution. Our lawyers claimed we got every penny back in restitution. It was about $2 million.

That sounded low to me. I figured they must have taken at least a few million more than that. The fraudulent contracts for the software research project were almost the full $2 million. I'm thinking there had to be at least a couple of million more skimmed from the building construction contracts and security firm contract. The most important thing, as I saw it, was that they were stopped before starting the really big spending on the ERCOT wholesale market overhaul and before taking anything nationwide.

I attended Steve's sentencing. Before the judge entered the courtroom, David Glickler pointed at me with a "You the man!" gesture.

Steve shuffled into the courtroom with a large neck brace from a fall he suffered while locked up. He looked totally broken, with slumped shoulders, three days without a shave, and the saddest-looking face. I bet he practiced that look in front of a mirror before entering the courtroom. He showed no remorse. Sobbing family members and friends gathered in support of Steve.

His attorney made one last plea for leniency. He claimed that the only way Steve could make good on his $800,000 restitution obligation was to take all the money out of his family's retirement funds. It was the last time I saw Steve. It was a great performance that I hoped would never have an encore.

After the sentencing, David thanked me for stepping up. It would be the last time I would see him too. It was another one of those lucky things for me that he had been assigned to this case.

David would then be assigned to create a new white-collar crimes division for the State of Texas.

Chris Uranga was tagged with a $500,000 restitution obligation. As far as I could tell, he was the only one convicted who felt remorse. He was last seen selling used cars at a dealership down the road from Taylor. He had been in way over his head with Ken.

As for Chris Douglas, I stopped feeling sorry for him when he was tagged with a $500,000 restitution obligation that went with his conviction. Apparently, he had been used in more than just the security incident. The $500,000 found in his possession was in transit to be used by others in Ken's inner circle. It appeared that Douglas had lost in a game of musical chairs. When the music stopped, he had no chair to sit in, only a large amount of money in his account that really didn't belong to him. It sucked for him. He was involved with musical chair professionals that had the game rigged in their favor.

As for Ken, he easily paid his $120,000 restitution obligation and certainly didn't feel any remorse. He did some jail time, then moved to California. I believe his wife went with him, but I couldn't confirm that. California was his new land of opportunity. Last I saw through the internet, he had his own consulting practice. I didn't think that his Texas experience would slow him down one bit. Ken was quite the character.

Tom, Margaret, and Maxine were exonerated of any wrongdoing. They were relieved that it was finally over, but the damage to their reputation was done.

Exoneration sounds good, but is only a legal term. It only signals the end of a life-draining experience. You could see it on the faces of Tom, Maxine, and Margaret. Their old habit of walking around with big smiles was gone.

As for me, the justice and exoneration were bittersweet. I was glad that the fraud was behind us, but the departure of Ken, Steve, and Uranga really didn't solve ERCOT's root problem of a huge opportunity for financial abuse. The quasi-governmental structure enabling The Stakeholders' Golden Rule remained firmly in place. Stay in your lane. No financial constraints. Only the best for the good people of Texas.

We still had all the ingredients for a perfect storm.

CONFIDENT IGNORANCE

38
Best in the World

It was a silent auction fundraiser. The affair was well-attended by all members of my division as well as friends from other ERCOT groups. The proceeds would go to James's family to help with his medical bills.

Cancer was eating away at James's body and he was taking large daily doses of pills with his chemotherapy. He didn't have much time left, and we all knew it. James was pretty weak but perked up a bit at the event. It was put together by his staff to celebrate his life and help his wife and two children with finances in their time of need.

It was really a celebration for all of us. The retail market project was completed under James's watch. There was still some synchronization testing required before the official cutover, but it was finished. There was no discussion about the ending of the Ken saga. Completion of the retail market project while James was still with us was a much more satisfying accomplishment than putting away a few crooks.

There were a lot of prizes contributed to the silent auction. A lot of restaurants and novelty gift shops had pitched in. There were gift baskets of wine and cheese and four admission tickets to Schlitterbahn, a waterpark in New Braunfels just south of Austin. The prize I bid on was a $100 gift certificate for sporting goods merchandise at Dick Powell's sporting goods outlet. I needed a new pair of golf shoes. I was happy to get it for $300. After the close of the auction, Jim congratulated me on the contribution. He had his eye on it but opted for a wine and cheese basket instead. He told me he was planning to buy a new bowling ball at Dick Powell's and that it was a great store inside the Taylor bowling alley. He didn't think they had golf shoes, but their bowling ball bags were pretty cool. I gave the certificate to Jim. I hadn't been bowling in thirty years.

There was a karaoke platform for those wanting to perform. The fee to perform went into the contribution fund. Others could contribute, too, if they wanted to entice a singer or had enjoyed the performance. It was a fun idea. The only problem for me was that I didn't recognize any of the songs. It must have been the dinosaur in me.

I was approached by one of my managers who said I should go up and sing "My Way" by Frank Sinatra. She felt it would be a perfect song for me to sing with words that defined the way James lived. Everyone knew that I never missed an opportunity to perform at a lunch and learn. This was an even better opportunity. My participation would certainly shake loose more contributions.

I declined because I felt that the affair was about James, not me or ERCOT management. I said "I'll contribute if someone else sings it." Of course, I missed the point. The event was for all of us. The party was a thank you to James from his staff, and it was to raise money for James's family. Much like kissing the pig, what better way to get contributions than to prop up the boss to let him embarrass himself? That's an expected part at these events. Perhaps it wasn't that big a deal, but I felt pretty bad about not participating. It still sticks out in my mind as a loss of an opportunity to further help James and the family.

The word about the success of our retail market overhaul spread quickly. Texas now owned the only truly deregulated retail electricity market in the world—a one-of-a-kind combination of business and technology that solved the toughest problems of retail deregulation. In addition, disputes went from a billion dollars to zero. There would be no more disputes.

However, to people outside the electric utility industry, it didn't seem like much of a big deal. It was ERCOT's job to resolve disputes, and the new retail provider switching process looked pretty easy to implement. So, what was the big deal?

Of course, that was precisely the big deal. Much like most noteworthy innovations, we created a simple solution to a complex problem. As for disputes, the big accomplishment was that we weren't getting any more disputes. They stayed at zero. The biggest intangible was the stakeholder satisfaction. Most were surprised that it worked and fit so well into the overall retail market process. My two blackballing stakeholder groups gave us two thumbs up. A small, yet pleasant surprise.

People inside the electric utility industry, both within the ERCOT stakeholder community and across the country, were quite impressed. We were now the industry leader in retail electricity deregulation. Whenever we attended industry meetings across the country, our peers picked our brains to learn how it worked. We even hosted visitors from overseas who wanted to find out more about what we had accomplished.

It really did become a worldwide showcase, a real quasi-governmental marvel. Other than the development of sophisticated surveillance tools and weapons for the military, governments rarely see such efficient and effective project execution and thorough results. My staff was quite proud. It was actually the most "feel good" accomplishment of my career.

There were still a few legislators and stakeholders pushing back on our success. They said it wasn't enough. It wasn't the completion of the exact task we were charged to implement through the deregulation legislation. Our work was viewed as an attempt to divert attention from the ultimate goal. They complained by asking the same old question. "Why haven't the six million-plus new automated real-time usage meters been procured, installed, and fully incorporated into the ERCOT system?"

We understood the need to keep our foot on the pedal to phase those in, but a little love at this point would have been much more appropriate. It certainly would have gone a long way toward bridging the gap between those legislators and ERCOT.

It was just not their nature. They never appreciated the need for the current work product to facilitate the larger technology implementation. It didn't bother us too much. They were politicians just being politicians. What did they know about such implementations? Nothing, of course. It was just politics. It was always politically correct to piss on ERCOT. They knew that there was nobody at ERCOT that would fight back. What they didn't see was that they simply weren't worth the effort for anyone to push back.

Because the retail market became a worldwide showcase for deregulation, I recommended we have our second new building dedicated to James. His name would be over the entrance as a reminder of his dedication and major contribution to ERCOT. There would be a plaque on the wall by the entrance telling James's story. Every new employee entering the building should strive to emulate his dedication and hard work. Why not? It made perfect sense.

It didn't fly. It was too big a stretch for our new chief executive officer, Tom Schrader, to appreciate James's work. Tom had only been at ERCOT a few weeks, and he had a lot of cultural changes to consider. Honoring one of the brightest and best who persevered through the toughest of personal challenges wasn't the cultural change he had in mind. When we discussed it, he was obviously more interested in the inventory of paper cups next to the coffee pot. "Why do we have medium-size cups?" he asked.

We settled on a bench crafted by one of James's project managers with a thank you to James inscribed on a gold plate attached to the backrest. It was a daily reminder to us of James's leadership and perseverance through adversity to achieve our goal.

39

Last Man Standing

The scam had been totally unmasked. Ken and his henchmen paid back about $2 million that was traced directly to them and did some jail time. ERCOT did its best to explain their deeds as a small rogue group of employees who were caught and brought to justice. Anyone who lived through the almost two years with them knew it was much more painful than the restitution and jail time might suggest.

The scandal took its toll on ERCOT officers and managers. There had been the expected purge; the departures were both voluntary and involuntary. Some were fired, others had had enough and wanted to move on. Still others saw their upward mobility stymied by the introduction of new officers brought in from outside of ERCOT. They needed to move on as well.

Obviously, Ken and his henchmen were gone. Tom Noel was gone. The once-proud, politically savvy former leader of the cutting-edge venture named ERCOT was now trying to cope with new feelings of disloyalty, disappointment, and bitterness that took hold of him during his final days at ERCOT.

Maxine was gone. She landed on her feet as a consultant in Houston. I believe her biggest takeaway was a feeling of relief. The farther back the scandal appeared in her rearview mirror, the closer it got to disappearing forever.

Gary, the human resources director with not enough time to do a background check on Steve, was gone. He had been with ERCOT from its start. His fate was the most unfair result of the wrongdoing and incompetence of others.

Margaret was gone. The transition must have been most uncomfortable for her. From what I gathered, she had believed that the quasi-governmental basics of ERCOT were a perfect match for what legislators wanted to do—an environment free from the burden of private investment shareholder responsibilities, an environment dedicated only to the common good and driven by an all-inclusive stakeholder process. She probably had it all figured out. I'm guessing she believed she had a perfect job doing exactly what she wanted to do. Unfortunately, she never factored in any risk associated with staying in her lane. She never factored in the consequences of her failure to include the protection of ERCOT from bad people as part of her lane. The scandal had to have eaten away at her personal life, as she found herself fighting a nasty divorce proceeding.

My pocket aces were gone—Jim and Rich had seen enough. They had accomplished a great deal, but there clearly was no upward mobility for them. It was time for them to move on. There was a sense of urgency. They needed to leverage their success before it got stale. I was thankful that they had stayed on board as long as they did. It's unlikely that I would have survived even three months of Ken without their hard work and unwavering support.

Rich joined a small solar energy-related company. He loved the smaller companies, particularly those with an equity ownership opportunity and a position to work with the founder to grow the business. He was brought in as a part owner for what was a residential solar panel business based in the Northeast, yet the position allowed Rich to stay and work out of Austin. It was a quality opportunity, right in Rich's wheelhouse.

Jim took a vice president position with one of ERCOT's electric generator stakeholder companies and moved to Dallas, where he did very well. But my perception was that his company underutilized his talent. That didn't matter too much to Jim, though. It was an officer position, and he was happy to get out from under the quasi-governmental governance.

I continued to see Jim quite a bit. He was that company's liaison to ERCOT's wholesale market overhaul project. At one point he and I were assigned to work on an overall plan to develop and implement that project. It was a tough assignment for him. As expected, my views conflicted with his company's views on project implementation, and Jim was caught in the middle. The good news for him was that the assignment didn't last very long. Our plan was rejected. More on that later.

Sam survived the purge. He was untouchable anyway. He was the stakeholders' surest bet to always "keep the fucking lights on." He appeared to be unaffected by the scandal. During his time as interim chief executive officer, he was dragged into a number of meetings, including depositions with the fraud suspects. He never shared anything about the attorney general's investigation. Like all of us, he was relieved that the ordeal was over.

A well-respected, long time representative from the Municipal Utility stakeholder group, Mark Dreyfus, began to refer to me as "the Last Man Standing." He said that I had been the odds-on favorite to be the first to go from Tom Noel's team when I was sent to the doghouse almost two years earlier by the two blackballing stakeholder groups. "You were a huge long shot to survive," Mark said to me. "Now you are to be known as 'the Last Man Standing.'" I hadn't thought of it that way. Not counting Sam, of course, it was true. It was also something to take some pride in, although I continued to feel the heat every day from the cauldron of tar and feathers being kept fresh and ready for use at a moment's notice by my critics.

Tom Noel came back for a visit with the new ERCOT officer group. He and his wife had been doing some traveling, including an eye-opening trip to China—the Great Wall, the Forbidden City, the Terracotta Army, and pandas were on their to-see list.

"If you ever go, remember to bring your own toilet paper," Tom said. "They don't produce enough, and what they have is not sanitary." Sage advice for sure, but a bit distasteful. For some reason, that comment stuck with me. I wondered if Tom might be losing it a little.

He appeared refreshed, though still a little upset that his tenure at ERCOT was highlighted by Ken's shenanigans. He couldn't get another gig. He only wanted one more chance for one more gig, but the stain of the ERCOT scandal was too visible to recruiters.

Sam and I were the only familiar faces in the room. At the beginning of the meeting, Tom Noel exchanged pleasantries with Sam. Then he sat down next to me. Our new chief executive officer, Tom Schrader, welcomed him back and pointed out how much we appreciated his leadership during such tumultuous times. The people in the room had no idea what he had been through. Use of the word *tumultuous* captured the woefully limited extent of their knowledge. It sounded both respectful and clueless.

Tom was coping pretty well with the disappointment and bitterness that highlighted his departure from ERCOT, but he apparently was not ready to forget the disloyalty. During a break in the meeting, Tom leaned over and looked me in the eye. "You know, Ray, I should have listened to you about Ken."

Duh! I knew that. At the time, Tom had to put his money on a sure thing, which was Ken, and not on a long shot like me. I said to him, "Thanks, Tom. A lot was swirling around those days. You did the best you could with the information you had at the time. I understood that." I wished him well.

At the end of the meeting, I stood in the gathering area outside the conference room listening to the buzz of conversations. I knew everybody there, but I was lonely. I was "Last Man Standing."

40
Brown Shoes

The end of the year brought hope and anticipation. The farmers of Taylor could prepare their fields for planting crops pretty early in the year. Corn and cotton fields would soon envelop farmhouses like a cozy warm blanket. Cattle grazed on that part of the farmland not suitable for planting. It was the livelihood for most residents in and around Taylor. Planting seeds gave them hope; daily weather reports fueled their anticipation.

The preparation and nurturing activities for a crop were straight out of an elementary school textbook. Tillage, then fertilizing, planting, and then, my favorite—crop-dusting. With work to do in fields on both sides of the road, small crop dusters flew over the highway to Taylor. They were entertaining for an old city boy like me. They flew low over the road, and you could see the pilot smiling. They looked like they were having way too much fun for it to be called work.

We were in crop-dusting mode at ERCOT. The weeds of fraudulent activity needed to be kept out of our field. A new ERCOT hotline was established for anonymous input for information about officer, manager, or any other employee wrongdoing. We would track down the slightest hint of fraudulent activity. I was happy with all of that. After the Ken affair, a new internal control was set forth in the ERCOT employee manual. One of the highlighted instructions to employees was to use the hotline to report anything they didn't want to see in the headline of a newspaper. A new employee today probably thinks that is funny. It certainly wasn't if you lived through it. Everybody expected that ERCOT would double down on its focus on internal controls. Obviously, we needed to be sure we didn't hire any more crooks.

The "bad guys" were gone.

All of ERCOT's dirty laundry had been tidily washed up. End of story, right?

Not quite.

What else could occur within the quasi-governmental environment to raise concerns about fiduciary responsibility? From where I sat, there was still plenty to worry about. I saw the Ken affair as a symptom of a much larger problem. Where there is an opportunity for fraud, there is an opportunity for financial abuse. That opportunity at ERCOT hadn't changed.

Unfortunately, nobody was willing to address the gaping hole of opportunity enabled by The Stakeholders' Golden Rule that was still very much a part of the ERCOT quasi-governmental environment. Millions of dollars could still make their way into sinkholes of opportunity baked into The Stakeholders' Golden Rule of no spending boundaries. It was the hope of all of us at ERCOT that a new officer team to join Sam and me would be well prepared to head off any brewing financial mishaps.

But it was the end of all worries for everyone else. Legislators and stakeholders seemed to treat the fraud as a tempest in a teapot. Embarrassing, yes, but nothing much more than that. We got our $2 million back, Ken and Steve were gone, and a new management team was in place. There was no need to read anything more into it.

What appeared to be the problem, the question of "What the hell is going on here?," was solved.

Of course, the *real* problem *wasn't* solved. It was the misguided trust in the utopian Stakeholders' Golden Rule that was the enabler. There were no practical limits on time or money to achieve the purely idealistic goal of the best interests of the public good. The opportunities for a breach of fiduciary responsibility were no different after the Ken affair than they were before he was hired. In fact, the false comfort from putting away the "bad guys" only resulted in a false conclusion that those opportunities were significantly reduced.

I wished I could have gotten comfortable working with the new unsuspecting ERCOT management team and the Alfred E. Neuman-like crowd of stakeholders, but it wasn't my nature. The size of that opportunity for financial abuse within the ERCOT quasi-governmental environment was as big as ever.

ERCOT was destined for a financial disaster far greater than the Ken affair. There would be no crooks. There would be no law-enforcement involvement. It would simply be a continuation of the dereliction of the duty to preserve the public trust in ERCOT.

There wasn't an internal control procedure anywhere in our quasi-governmental stakeholder-driven process that would mitigate the opportunity for financial negligence due to the utopian Stakeholders' Golden Rule. With confident ignorance, hundreds of millions of dollars would be dumped into a sinkhole. Then stakeholders would pat themselves on the back for a job well done. It would be both entertaining and intellectually exhausting.

My status at ERCOT would undergo a significant change—not involving my position or my responsibilities, but my perspective. Instead of working as the "go to" businessperson, I would be on the outside looking in.

The blackballing stakeholders always kept me outside the stakeholder inner circle. But personally, and professionally, I fit in pretty well with Tom, Sam, Margaret, and Maxine. We were a good team except for the "stay in your lane" concept. We held each other's opinions in high regard.

It was different now. As the new team came on board one by one, it appeared to me that I wouldn't fit in with them at any level. They believed that they were the business experts and my input was of marginal value.

It was my new perspective. As George Gobel once said on the *Tonight Show Starring Johnny Carson*, "Did you ever get the feeling that the world is a tuxedo and you're a pair of brown shoes?"

That is how I felt. It did give me more time to paint the pictures of the new ERCOT realities from that new perspective. My pictures would be far more entertaining and far less serious than my grand jury masterpiece.

41

Into a Perfect Storm

Sam and I welcomed our new chief executive officer, Tom Schrader. I called a former client of mine who had worked under Tom a few years before Tom was hired by ERCOT. Tom had been promoted to be his boss, so I expected some honest insight into working with Tom. I was told that Tom was known in his previous leadership position as being a real "Boy Scout." That meant that he was trustworthy, loyal, helpful, friendly, courteous, kind, obedient, cheerful, thrifty, brave, clean, and reverent. Hmmm. Nothing in there about competent, politically savvy, or street-smart. I would have to give him some rope to see what he would do with it.

Tom was a good person as well as an honest one. A Princeton engineer and seasoned natural gas utility executive, I thought he was a pretty good hire on paper. The board of directors thought so too. It is so hard to get the right fit from a resume and a couple of interviews. To their credit, they did perform a background check on him before he was extended an offer.

I had some concerns. First, even though he came with stakeholder approval, it was highly likely that he would have a rough time working with them. There was a general view taken by electric utility people, like the stakeholders at ERCOT, that the natural gas utility business was a weak sibling to their more complex business of "keeping the lights on." How things were done in the natural gas utility business was rarely accepted as transferable to electric utility operations. Second, he was a "for profit" corporate guy. It didn't matter how much experience he had interacting with a Public Utility Commission in rate cases; the quasi-governmental environment and the stakeholder process would feast on his lack of experience in dealing with their unique challenges.

My third concern showed up shortly after he came on board. Tom was committed to a 10 percent reduction in costs every year. He claimed it to be the Six Sigma management approach. Unfortunately, it was a misuse of the guidelines set forth in the Six Sigma theory. Six Sigma was an engineering approach, not a management approach. It was intended only as a means to eventually reduce production defects to zero in a manufacturing process. I wished Tom had gotten his MBA after Princeton to clarify his understanding of the difference between engineering techniques and business leadership initiatives.

ERCOT operating costs were approved annually by the Public Utility Commission. Through the commission's approval process, we were already under close public scrutiny. We didn't need to compound the challenges of that close public scrutiny with a misapplication of an engineering technique to theoretically take ERCOT operating costs to zero.

It wasn't that big a deal. We could all probably find ways to cut costs. Not 10 percent a year, of course, but an annual review similar to zero-based budgeting was a reasonable exercise. The whole Six Sigma thing set unreasonable expectations of our critics, the Public Utility Commissioners, and our board of directors. We could have gotten along just fine without it.

With such a big emphasis on reducing operating costs, it was a huge surprise to me that Tom bought in to The Stakeholders' Golden Rule of no capital spending constraints. Much like the administration before him, he deemed that to be a combined Public Utility Commission and stakeholder responsibility and not a concern for ERCOT management. The gaping hole of opportunity for fraud and financial wrongdoing was not an issue for Tom. We would focus on much more important things under our direct control. He and I got off to a bit of a bumpy start on that one. You know that the opportunity for financial fraud and dereliction of duty were my pet peeves.

Tom's cost-cutting focus was more annoying than it was a burden. He hosted his first ERCOT holiday dinner event in December 2005, shortly after he was hired. He implemented a pricing glitch that made employees take notice. Water and iced tea were free, but after-dinner coffee was four dollars per cup. Really.

To make his desire for a cost-cutting culture change perfectly clear, Tom's first official move was to reduce our inventory of Styrofoam coffee cups. He said that we didn't need medium and large cups, only small cups. I had to think about that one for a while. Over the long run, would that be a real cost saving?

I decided to continue to give Tom the benefit of any doubts until I met the replacements he had for Maxine and Ken.

Our new chief financial officer, Steve Byone, was a piece of work. He had a long list of new internal controls that wouldn't stop the bleeding of even the slightest paper cut. The big picture of ERCOT's quasi-governmental opportunistic structure and welcoming call of The Stakeholders' Golden Rule for fraud and financial wrongdoing weren't his problem. He wanted to be sure we covered all the bases in the weeds.

The new chief information officer, Ron Hinsley, had his most relevant experience working in Australia. Everyone thought it was cool that he worked in Australia. His accomplishments there seemed mostly as an observer instead of as a doer, but, hey, he worked in Australia! It had to be a good experience. Ron had never implemented a large information technology software application project to completion. In fact, he had very little experience with such activities. Stakeholders didn't care about that. He would eventually oversee the ERCOT wholesale market overhaul implementation.

Ron's resume showed that he had a college degree from a school in Nebraska. He let everyone assume he graduated from the University of Nebraska. Having lived through the background check problems with our previous chief information officer, I looked up the school he actually attended. It was an all-female school with a total enrollment of about five hundred students. I had nothing against an all-female school, but how did it make any sense that Ron would have attended that school? And it was not the University of Nebraska.

He had a "technology drives business" approach that was no different than Ken's. Another one of my pet peeves. I know what you are thinking, I wouldn't like our new chief information officer even if his name was Bill Gates instead of Ron Hinsley. Could be, I guess.

Tom brought in a new in-house counsel. She never said too much. She always seemed bored at management committee meetings, but she never seemed concerned about any senseless sermon on cost cutting or internal controls. ERCOT was only a pit stop for her. She spent most of her time looking for a better opportunity.

Tom completed his staff by making the human resources position a new officer-level job. Like the chief information technology position, having an officer-level human resources person was a disturbing national trend. It should be a support position to the leading dogs and not another leading dog—just something else I had to accept and try to make work.

The woman hired by Tom into the job was really good—well-qualified, smart, and helpful. Unfortunately, she only stayed a few months. She took another position returning to the more familiar "for profit" corporate environment.

Her replacement was not a good hire, in my opinion. She had an irritating, antagonistic manner and a destructive personal agenda that occasionally made its way into our activities.

The new officers flooded Tom with senseless concerns and useless information. To his credit, Tom never overreacted. He knew that Sam and I had things under control. Overall, the new team was weak and certainly not as good as what we had before, but, as far as I knew at that point, none of them were crooks.

The new team was a key piece of a new perfect storm. Weak ERCOT players. Strong opposition to ERCOT in general due to the fraud activities. A virtual blank check issued by the Public Utility

Commission for the new ERCOT wholesale market overhaul project. A stakeholder cultlike following of The Stakeholders' Golden Rule. The quasi-governmental nonsense of "staying in your lane." Worst of all, for me, there was still a target on my back that was always in the sights of the shotguns pointed at me by the leaders of the blackballing independent generator and energy marketer stakeholder groups.

I braced for another wild ride.

42

The Proof of the Pudding
Is in the Eating

A key lesson I learned early in my career in the software development business is that working smarter instead of harder is the key ingredient in every successful technology project. Unfortunately, working smarter instead of harder was not one of the guiding principles of any of my new peers or the ERCOT stakeholder groups.

Voicing my concern about that, as it applied to the ERCOT wholesale market overhaul project, fell on deaf ears. The two blackballing stakeholder groups couldn't care less. They used it to paint another picture, once again, to push me out of those activities. It evolved through the high-profile next step for ERCOT wholesale market overhaul project.

The stakeholder discussions about the ERCOT wholesale market overhaul were in full swing. The Public Utility Commission had issued its order for change. The ERCOT stakeholder decision was to create a unique ERCOT wholesale market platform with all the bells and whistles Texas consumers deserved.

At its core, it would simply replace bundled generating unit bids and the rules of thumb used by Sam's folks to select generating units. They would instead select individual generating units based on the results of an optimization decision support tool.

The optimization approach proposed for use by ERCOT was similar to the optimization approach used in the natural gas industry. It had already been implemented successfully at four other ERCOT-like power pools. The implementation was not a bleeding-edge technology challenge. It was a complex business implementation.

Given the success of the retail market overhaul, I was asked to work with a small task force to come up with a high-level approach and cost estimate for the ERCOT wholesale market overhaul project. My old friend and colleague, Jim, was asked to work with me. It was good news for me, but bad news for Jim.

We would propose working smarter instead of harder. Jim had been a key player, along with James, in our successful phased-in approach on the ERCOT retail market overhaul and believed in the merits of that approach. He was torn between his respect for my opinion and his boss's strong dislike of me. Jim could only hold his breath and wait until we finished our work. At least it was an opportunity to get my thoughts out there, and on the record. We both knew that there was no way anything I recommended would be adopted.

We paddled feverishly upstream against a strong stakeholder current of disdain over my participation. The success of the retail market overhaul project didn't matter to them. Jim's boss and his blackballing stakeholder brethren made sure that stakeholders were onboard with that. They would argue that the ERCOT wholesale market overhaul was completely different and much more complex than simple accounting challenges addressed in the retail market overhaul. Jim and I expected their pushback but didn't try to factor those politics into our proposal. We put together what we believed to be the best plan.

As with the retail market overhaul, Jim and I came up with a phased-in approach to implement the necessary ERCOT wholesale market modifications and keep the existing processes that still would be needed. We had determined that to start from scratch would be unnecessary and much too risky. Starting with a whiteboard on an open-ended project like this would take too long and cost too much. It was our recommendation to work smarter rather than harder. Our cost estimate was $75 million to complete a two-year, phased-in ERCOT wholesale market overhaul project.

Jim's boss and the other blackballing stakeholders hit the roof. How could I suggest such an outrageous number? They declared that the estimate was way too high. There was no way the project would cost anywhere near that much. They would be pretty assertive with their concern. Their complaint to Tom went something like this: "Clearly, Ray is trying to kill the effort with an inflated cost estimate. No way the project will cost that much! Ray needs to be removed from an overall project-leadership position."

Tom was bombarded with similar complaints. He was assured he wouldn't survive if I stayed in the loop. Nobody knew exactly what he was being told, but, years later, he would be quoted about the project in an article in an industry publication. Tom's exact words were, "The stakeholders' reaction to Ray's proposal was very violent."

Toast again. The "Last Man Standing" was now teetering on his last leg. It didn't hurt my feelings. I knew that people usually get what they ask for. These stakeholders would get what they wanted.

Nobody blamed Jim, but I still felt bad for him. He treated it like a bad round of golf. No excuses. No pouting. Stakeholder respect for him never wavered. He could get back to enjoying his real job. And he was still a good friend.

Stakeholders initiated a made-from-scratch ERCOT wholesale market overhaul project. It would exploit the widest of all the possible gaping-hole opportunities for seemingly innocent financial wrongdoing by good people. Gluttony, wrath, pride, envy, and greed came to mind. I was guessing that stakeholders believed that they were such good people that they had a special exemption from those five of the seven deadly sins. Probably not, but they certainly were enthusiastic about their blank check to work harder, not smarter.

I took a ringside seat. We'd see how it would play out. One thing was certain—the proof of the pudding would be in the eating.

Let's eat.

43

We Don't Need
No Stinkin' Results

My recommended approach was evolution. Stakeholders didn't want any thinking along the lines of an evolution. They wanted revolution.

They decided that there was not enough detailed information in the Public Utility Commission rule about the overhaul to create an overall upfront plan. Such a rush to judgment would be imprudent. They had gotten through the Public Utility Commission hearings that produced an order telling ERCOT what to do. They reminded themselves of what the next step should be. They would have to come up with a completely new script of protocols for the new ERCOT wholesale market. They had to scrap all the existing protocols.

They would start with a whiteboard. An outside consultant, Trip Doggett, was asked to facilitate those stakeholder activities. Trip was a stakeholder darling and an outside consultant whom everybody knew was a religious follower of The Stakeholders'

Golden Rule. There would be no entries on the whiteboard based on a rush to judgment. Time was not a constraint. It was only about the best for Texas consumers who never wanted an ERCOT wholesale market overhaul in the first place.

A voting process was set up in an effort to move forward issu by issue on a new design. A new task force was created. That effort was the Texas Nodal Task Force, appropriately referred to as "TNT" in shorthand.

The stakeholders were concerned that the notion of fiduciary responsibility might creep into the minds of some of their con-stituents. Some in their ranks might get a twinge of conscience. To cover that base, the first order of business for TNT was a tacit approval of a strict adherence to The Stakeholders' Golden Rule for the entire ERCOT wholesale market overhaul project. From their first meeting, it was clear that the process would never be impeded due to a rush for results or limit on spending, either or both of which would only yield a less-than-optimal result. Texans would have only the best. That was the extent of the TNT fidu-ciary responsibility. The TNT could continue its activities until hell froze over. There would be no individual stakeholder exposures to financial irresponsibility.

As Steve Wolens might have told us, the only thing at risk was the professional survival of ERCOT employees. That was an out-come that only the employees of ERCOT would have to deal with, not the stakeholders. It was all about pursuing the very best for Texas consumers at the risk of ERCOT employees who had noth-ing to do with the process!

The first task was to create a completely new set of ERCOT wholesale market protocols, and it was up to the TNT to determine how to do it. There could be no ERCOT wholesale market overhaul project plan without the new set of protocols.

Some stakeholders laughingly claimed that their stakeholder process to create those protocols was like making sausage. Trying to make something edible by grinding together ingredients that would otherwise have no culinary value sounded about right. Others, who became frustrated from time to time, said it was like watching paint dry. They had used those clichés before for pretty much all stakeholder and Public Utility Commission hearing activities.

This was different. It had all the entertainment value of a three-ring circus. It would give the master showman, P. T. Barnum, a run for his money. ERCOT staff members, though, totally at risk for the outcome, were in for a treat. The protocol-development circus would wind up being in town with varying forms of stakeholder entertainment for more than a year!

The show started every morning with the stakeholders driving up to our facility. It was like having little Volkswagens descending on our building and then a whole bunch of clowns jumping out. Yes. They were all well-meaning good people and not clowns, but, after all, you need to get the true feeling of the experience. Let me paint the picture.

They gathered in the large hallway outside the main meeting room in preparation for each day's events. It was like being backstage before a big performance. Everyone appeared to be rehearsing. You could smell the presence of a number of elephants in the room—each stakeholder group had its own agenda.

Once inside, Trip Doggett, the stakeholder darling and TNT ringleader, called the meeting to order. Each stakeholder group communicated their views through various schticks. Their approaches to make its points were unique circus-like routines—high-wire acts, acrobats, and even contortionists.

My favorites were the animal tamers—my independent generator and energy marketer blackballing stakeholder groups. They would yell, crack their whips, and chase the wild beasts until they obeyed. There was no middle ground. They would never let any of the stakeholders' animals get the upper hand. It was their way or the highway.

At the end of each day, the stakeholders gathered for the final act. It became a tradition. A guest, representing Texas consumers, would attend and be given a $500 coupon just for participating in the grand finale. It was only good when applied to a switch of their electric service to any retail electric provider of their choice.

I had to admit, it was pretty entertaining.

After more than a year, the circus of protocol debates was as popular as ever. It got rave reviews from, you guessed it, almost every stakeholder group. The only reason the protocol effort ended was because the Public Utility Commission demanded that stakeholders shut down the circus—a rare departure from Public Utility Commission standard procedure. The stakeholders probably would still be debating protocol details but for the demand of the commissioners to cease and desist.

You would think that an effort of more than a year's duration that produced still-incomplete protocols would be a red flag that the ensuing implementation effort might be mess.

How could it turn into a mess? Stakeholders had religiously followed the quasi-governmental requirements of collaboration and process. Every stakeholder had been included. Everybody was in the boat. Everybody was getting what they wanted.

Besides that, there was The Stakeholders' Golden Rule. They had complied with, it as well, during that effort. They had avoided the pressure for results that could only ensure suboptimal solutions. They pursued an outcome that would surely be in the very best interests for Texas consumers. The Stakeholders' Golden Rule was beginning to grow on me: "Results? Results? We don't need no stinkin' results."

Even better was the fact that the cost attributed to the ERCOT wholesale market overhaul project for that more than one-year effort was considered to be *zero*, and the project implementation plan was still a whiteboard. There was no stakeholder remorse, just accolades for their accomplishment to date.

After the instruction from the Public Utility Commission to move on, stakeholders told Tom how ERCOT should proceed with the implementation phase of the ERCOT wholesale market overhaul project. There would be a new stakeholder task force facilitated by Trip Doggett—the ERCOT Nodal Transition Plan Task Force, or "TPTF." Why not? After all, according to stakeholders, TNT had worked so well. Why not continue the same process under a name that sounded like they were making progress?

ERCOT's chief information officer, Ron Hinsley, would be the ERCOT implementation leader. Remember his resume? He had never completed a software application project in his life. I guessed stakeholders thought this would be a good project on which he could cut his teeth. They knew he never heard of fiduciary responsibility. They knew he would be happy to always do what stakeholders told him to do. They knew he believed he could never be fired for that.

Ron had no clue what to do, so he did what any other chief information officer would do. He brought in an outside contractor, Kathy Hager, to lead the implementation. She appeared to have reasonable project implementation experience, but not for something as politically charged as this.

She vowed to be tough with stakeholders to get results. I knew that wouldn't happen. Stakeholders kept telling her that it was about process, not results. She tried to push back to meet some planned project milestones. She just didn't get it.

"Results? Results? We don't need no stinkin' results."

44

Thinking Outside the Box

The stakeholders deemed it appropriate for me to keep the responsibility for completion of the settlements and billing piece of the ERCOT wholesale market overhaul project.

Kathy noted that my staff had a proven track record working well with Ron's staff to get things done. We were interested in results, so she gave us free rein to implement as we saw fit, separate from the "we keep the lights on" portion of the ERCOT wholesale market overhaul project. She assigned a project manager from her pool of outside consultants to work with us and had that person keep her posted on our progress. We all worked well together.

Surprisingly, my approach for the settlements and billing piece came under immediate criticism from Nancy Capezzuti, our vice president of human resources. Yes, Nancy, our VP for *human resources* telling me that my approach to the implementation of the new settlements and billing system was unacceptable. Truly a knuckleheaded move on her part.

Nancy's husband was a local customer representative for one of the largest worldwide providers of big computer and data storage. And because of that, apparently, she believed he knew everything about software implementations. We hired him briefly to comment to the board of directors on our project.

Nancy's husband recommended that ERCOT place their trust in a project outsourced to a worldwide leader in such implementations. He would be happy to share with us how his company would approach such a task.

Their approach was to deploy an army of PMPs (project management professionals) to build the system to our specifications. After the system was built, additional PMPs would come in to train our people on how to operate their one-of-a-kind system. They would then contract with us to provide maintenance, support, and additional training services as needed in the future.

It sounded simple. It was an accepted approach followed by electric utility operations staffs around the world. That was the approach already being used by Kathy for Sam's part of the ERCOT wholesale market overhaul project.

I had seen too many projects that accepted that PMP approach turn into disasters. Those projects got started and were quickly infested with PMPs. They turned into bottomless pits of expenditures with no project end in sight. I wanted to use a better approach to implement my settlements and billing portion of the ERCOT wholesale market overhaul project. Fortunately, Kathy didn't push back. As Ron's overall project manager for the ERCOT wholesale market overhaul, she could have insisted on the more conventional approach. Instead, Kathy instructed one of her PMPs to follow my lead to run with it my way.

My approach was different. I outsourced a project to consultants to assume the routine day-to-day activities of my staff. I had my staff train those outside consultants on how to perform their routine day-to-day activities. I then redirected *my staff* to manage the development and implementation of the new system we needed for the ERCOT wholesale market overhaul settlements and billing functions.

Our approach was focused on delivering results in the most efficient and effective manner. My staff would design and manage the implementation. There was no need for my staff to try to document specifications in enough detail for a third-party consultant to figure out what we needed. There would be no costly and time-consuming circling in loops of misunderstood instructions.

Upon completion, my staff would be immediately ready to run the new system. They wouldn't need to be trained in the use of the new system. They had already designed it and managed its implementation. They knew how it worked.

We would discharge the outside consultants working on our old routine day-to-day activities when we cut over to the implementation of the new system. When we hired new employees down the road, my staff would train them. We wouldn't have to pay for any additional outside consulting help.

We would have no part of any PMP infestation.

The problem, for me, was that Nancy claimed that my approach to implement the settlements and billing piece of the

ERCOT wholesale market project conflicted with the best practices used by the large companies like her husband's. She cried foul and took her case to Tom. How could ERCOT justify paying consultants to do our repetitive daily routine tasks? Where were the PMPs to develop the new system? She believed that I had to be violating some legislative or Public Utility Commission rules.

I got lucky. Tom chose to ignore her and trust my judgment.

As you might expect, our group was ready to cut over to the new ERCOT wholesale market settlements and billing platform more than eighteen months before there was even any talk of any ERCOT wholesale market overhaul project end in sight. Our task was easier than the "keeping the lights on" task, but not that much easier. The difference was the focus on results. Just like our retail market overhaul project, we were able to avoid any stakeholder concerns about violating The Stakeholders' Golden Rule. We went a different way because we *wanted and delivered* stinkin' results!

45

PMPs Everywhere

The attempt to implement the "keeping the lights on" portion of the ERCOT wholesale market overhaul project proved to be more entertaining than the one-year-plus protocol development phase. It wasn't a circus. It was a high-energy trip into Never Never Land. More often than not, it appeared to have no adult supervision.

Information technology people, engineers, subject matter experts, and, best of all, PMPs were everywhere. These were highly trained people, certified as alleged experts in project management.

PMPs had an interesting history. They were a brainchild of that same worldwide consulting firm that began recommending and placing chief information officers in corporations. The use of PMPs solidified an almost exclusive sales channel for that firm and other similar firms positioned to deliver such business/information technology services.

Chief information officers could fill a major void in their information technology expertise by hiring PMPs. These were brought in as unique business/technology project management specialists. They were engaged as experts in implementing technology applications for business users to be ultimately served by the chief information officer. The PMPs populated their project teams with staff from their same consulting firm.

PMPs were not to be confused with *pimps*. Pimps were project managers in what we generally refer to as the world's oldest profession—prostitution. PMPs were associated with what most businesspeople referred to as the world's second-oldest profession—consulting. However, they shared disturbing similarities that caused many to view them as the same.

The high-level similarity is that the job of both pimps and PMPs is to get the highest possible revenue from a client through the promise of the highest level of customer satisfaction. Efficient and effective delivery is not part of the equation. As you can see, that approach fit perfectly with the ERCOT Stakeholders' Golden Rule, but it did create confusion for Ron as to whether he was getting results or just getting pimped.

There is no confusing their approaches, but the job of PMPs and pimps is the same. Pimps use glitz and fear as their primary sales tools. PMPs use kindness and tact to sell more business. Both are targeted at shaking down the client for as much money as possible.

They both begin their work with a reasonable cost estimate. We are never exactly sure what that buys us, but we are guaranteed full satisfaction delivered by proven professionals. In our pent-up desire to get started, we don't pay much attention to the details. We contract for the work, agreeing to pay the initial cost estimate.

Both continue their work asking us to describe in greater detail what we want. Pimps call it "a hustle." PMPS call it "a statement of work." That translates into a plan, including a general outline of the tasks and a revised, fine-tuned cost estimate. There is, of course, the ongoing assurance of full satisfaction. The fine-tuned cost estimate is always higher than the initial cost estimate. Our pent-up desire for satisfaction leads to our agreement to pay the higher cost for the alleged final statement of work. Money exchanges hands to seal the deal.

Shortly after beginning the project, we find that we require deviations from the plan to fulfill our increasing desire for satisfaction. We need to review and revise the statement of work before going any further. Obviously, there is an increase in the cost estimate to account for the extra effort.

This can happen a number of times before we realize our dilemma. We have committed to an endless cycle of clarifying needs, time delays, and increased costs. We can: (a) accept it and, with ongoing assurance of full satisfaction, just continue to pay and make believe we expected it all along; (b) get angry, realize we have paid quite a bit already, think about how we don't want to lose it, then accept it, and just continue to pay with ongoing assurance of full satisfaction; or, (c) we can cancel the effort, but why would we do that when we have come so far and paid so much with not much further to go?

Typically, at this point there is cause for concern. The buy-in has gotten much too large. We are either afraid to argue with the pimp or afraid to go to our boss and admit that we made a huge mistake hiring PMPs.

The implementation of the ERCOT wholesale market overhaul project had PMPs everywhere. Managed by ERCOT Chief Information Officer Ron Hinsley, stakeholders bought into the approach. PMPs fit perfectly in the ERCOT governance environment. Their financial opportunity widens automatically without boundaries to meet their demands. The quasi-governmental environment protects ERCOT management from fiduciary responsibility. The Stakeholders' Golden Rule enables PMPs to ply their trade without timeline or budget concerns. It all happens with the guarantee of full satisfaction, which is defined as the best result for Texas consumers. There can be no losers except ERCOT management.

Totally honest. Totally legal. No financial constraints. Just the promise of full satisfaction. I can't remember ever being more entertained in a professional environment.

The cost estimate for the completion of the overhaul project quickly reached $125 million. Soon after that, there was a revised estimate of $263 million. That didn't count what was spent on the one-year-plus protocol-definition phase or what stakeholders were spending on their own getting ready for the changes they had to make on their end.

It didn't bother Ron. Stakeholders still loved him. He assumed he could avoid any blame. That was why he hired Kathy Hager, his overall PMP. And, if needed, he could always point to me as a key player in undermining the progress of the project. Nobody would ask how that might be happening. They would simply accept the assertion. Stakeholders loved hearing that kind of shit.

Kathy knew that the ERCOT wholesale market overhaul project was out of control. She also knew she was on the hot seat. She came to me and said, "I'm concerned but have no one to talk to. Can you help me?"

Like I did with Kevin Judice and Mike Pettersen before her, I listened to Kathy's concern. She wanted at least one ERCOT officer to support her push for stakeholders to compromise to get results. But, as was the case with Kevin, I couldn't help. She was applying pressure on stakeholders on certain issues to be able to get the project done. All they did was either push back or ignore her request. ERCOT staff wasn't supporting her in that effort. She needed officer help.

I told her that she would never get anybody at ERCOT to pressure stakeholders. I said, "I'm not surprised ERCOT staff is ignoring your request for that kind of help. Any hint of even talking about such a thing would probably get them fired. You need to find some other way to influence stakeholders. We don't do the 'telling,' we 'do what we are told to do.'" I had waited a long time to finally tell somebody that. Kathy was angry and disappointed. She wanted my help. I told her that I wouldn't. It would only make things worse if I got involved. She seemed lost and defeated when she left my office.

Our board of directors and the Public Utility Commission were getting nervous. Commissioners wanted answers. Kathy was on the hot seat. She had no answers as to why the project appeared out of control. She was reduced to tears and resigned.

Ron brought in a replacement. Lou Costello (not really his name, but it should have been, considering the comedic atmosphere) came in to give it a try. The ERCOT wholesale market overhaul was left to chug away under the still enthusiastic guidance of Ron and the bemused leadership of Lou Costello. To this day, I think Lou is still trying to figure out what's on second, despite still not knowing who's on first. That's an old, worn-out routine, but, again, I think you get the picture.

The fallout from the opportunity given to PMPs would ultimately be worse than the hiring of Ken Shoquist and his con men.

Honest, hardworking PMPs were everywhere. Doing a magnificent job. Making a lot of money. Delivering interim results that required more modifications. They feasted on the ERCOT wholesale market overhaul project. They were unencumbered and protected by stakeholders under the guarantee of no limits and "only the best for Texas consumers."

46

Bartender, I'll Have Another Chief Executive Officer, Please

It was no surprise when Tom resigned. His fate had been sealed when stakeholders refused to allow him to control the ERCOT wholesale market overhaul project.

His departure was an easy call for the Public Utility Commission, legislators, and our board of directors. There was the steep increase in the estimated cost of the ERCOT wholesale market overhaul project and the growing uncertainty of its completion date. In addition, ERCOT still hadn't implemented the six million-plus automated real-time usage meters into their retail market. ERCOT was again too far off track.

I suspected that there was a little more to it. While not privy to any such exchange, Tom might have wanted to tell the Public Utility Commission and our board that stakeholders were getting exactly what they wanted. They controlled those problems and faithfully applied The Stakeholders' Golden Rule to their control.

The proof of the pudding was in the eating, and they were eating so fast and so much that they were about to explode.

Stakeholders were well aware of that situation. They couldn't let Tom have time to make such an argument. Tom had to go, and they had to take control of the chief executive officer position.

Once again, Sam and I temporarily took charge of our respective day-to-day responsibilities. Sam continued to have a stakeholder pass regarding any responsibility for the "keeping the lights on" part of the ERCOT wholesale market overhaul project. It still had a long way to go. Stakeholders knew that he wasn't going to get involved. They would be safe again with Tom out of the picture.

It seemed to me that completion of the project should be at the top of the list for the new chief executive officer. The legislators had to be concerned. And it appeared that the Public Utility Commissioners were getting pretty uncomfortable with the ERCOT requests for huge increases of debt. They all hoped for a new chief executive officer who could find the root cause of the ERCOT wholesale market overhaul project overrun, stop the bleeding, and finish it.

But our board of directors had a little different view of the ERCOT situation. Any vote of the board of directors was controlled by a 70 percent majority populated by stakeholder representatives. That majority had too much invested already in the status quo of adherence only to the desires of stakeholders and The Stakeholders' Golden Rule. Our all-inclusive, quasi-governmental governance structure gave those stakeholders the control to bring in one of their own. There would be no change in the status quo.

The stakeholder majority argued that Tom, a product of the private corporate environment, obviously didn't work. There was no time to experiment with another CEO from that world. They had to have a person with quasi-governmental experience who could hit the ground running while abiding by The Stakeholders' Golden Rule. ERCOT must remain steadfast in the pursuit of the very best for Texas consumers. The new chief executive officer must be committed to that pursuit, and there was no need to start cutting corners. ERCOT's job was still about doing what stakeholders told it to do. The new chief executive officer had to have compliance with that requirement as part of his or her DNA.

The board of directors hired one of their own. Bob Kahn replaced Tom. Bob was the longtime ERCOT board member from the municipal utility stakeholder group. He was literally one of their own.

Bob had extensive experience working with ERCOT. That background was viewed as a big plus by the board of directors. He was a lawyer by training, with a specialty in human resources legal matters. He was a career public power guy with no "for profit" executive tendencies.

Bob's understanding of fiduciary responsibility within the ERCOT quasi-governmental environment was exactly the same as Margaret's original understanding. The stakeholder protocols controlled ERCOT operations, and the newly adopted ERCOT wholesale market stakeholder protocols controlled the ERCOT wholesale market overhaul project. Just like Margaret, he believed that it should be easy—just do what you are told. In addition, he was completely at ease with endless processes. No way he could be fired by his stakeholder colleagues by letting the stakeholder process run its course for the ERCOT wholesale market overhaul project. I could hear Bob saying to himself, "It's so easy. What, me worry?"

About five-foot-nine with a medium build, Bob had dark black hair and a large fuzzy black moustache. He was quiet and had no obvious "tells" about his emotions.—a real poker player. In fact, he loved going by himself to The Venetian hotel and resort in Las Vegas just to play poker for a few days. According to the rumor mill, his wife gave him a pass to make those trips three or four times a year. It was one of those spouse stories I found hard to believe. In any event, Bob was always hard to read.

Stakeholders wanted to be sure that Bob would let the stakeholder process run its course. They had some concern that Bob had been the board member representing the municipal utility stakeholder group that never wanted the ERCOT wholesale market overhaul. He assured the board of directors that he would neither push for a stop of the ERCOT wholesale market overhaul project nor push for an arbitrary premature finish of the project. He would let it run its course.

Bob got the job as well as the approval of the board of directors to hire a new chief operating officer to oversee the implementation of the ERCOT wholesale market overhaul implementation. He would also oversee Sam and me. That would require some adjustments for us. We had worked well together for five years navigating what we thought were pretty challenging times.

It clearly signaled the end for both of us. There would be too many chiefs. We would have a chief executive officer, chief operating officer, chief of grid operations, chief of market operations, and chief information officer. It wasn't too hard to figure it out. Sam was respected by stakeholders but figured to be retiring soon. The new chief operating officer would assume his responsibilities. The new chief operating officer could probably assume my responsibilities as well. I needed to be promoted to chief operating officer or be gone.

Sam had been through two rotations as interim chief executive officer. He had seen enough and had accomplished a great deal. He wasn't going to work for Bob. He was senior to Bob when they both worked for the same public power entity. Sam would stick around a little longer to mentor Bob and the new chief operating officer, then leave.

Bob had assured the board of directors that the new chief operating officer candidate would get their required approval prior to extending an offer. The new chief operating officer would do what stakeholders told him or her to do. The job specification was clear. It had to be a proven stakeholder darling.

The hiring process would be only for optics. Bob and the stakeholder members of the board of directors already knew who that would be. Bob would go through the motions of interviewing a cross section of qualified candidates. He took some time to decide on his pick, to keep up the appearance of a fair and open process.

I was scheduled to interview for the job. The Public Utility Commissioners and our unaffiliated board members actually thought I was a bona fide candidate. They didn't know the fix was in. The pictures of me that were painted by the stakeholders about my five years with ERCOT portrayed a number of impressions of me. Some were positive, but most were negative. And *stakeholder darling* certainly wasn't among them.

47
Greasing the Skids

Bob hired what would be the fifth in-house legal counsel to serve at ERCOT since I arrived. His name was Mike. I never could remember his last name. Being Bob's first officer hire placed him clearly in Bob's inner circle. He seemed to fit pretty well with Steve, Nancy, and Ron. In my mind's eye, they were a bit like the Three Stooges (Mo, Larry, Curly) plus Shemp.

Tom's resignation spawned an action item tied to it by the Public Utility Commission. For whatever reason, they felt that they had to do something more than simply settle on a new chief executive officer.

They were worried about ERCOT's habit of appearing to outsiders as being financially derelict in their duties. They needed to do something to show legislators and public advocates that they were still engaged in ERCOT intendance. The Public Utility Commission hired a consulting firm to talk with ERCOT officers and make recommendations on operating cost-saving improvements.

I was a little surprised again. The review would ignore the entire ERCOT wholesale market overhaul project and The Stakeholders' Golden Rule. It was to focus on the issue of having too many "chiefs" in the officer ranks. With a chief operating officer, we would be too top-heavy.

I knew that the ERCOT wholesale market overhaul project was the big kahuna. Our board of directors could handle the "too many chiefs" issue. No need for trying to kill that fly with a sledgehammer.

Rather than just telling us to fire a couple of our "chiefs," they brought in consultants allegedly to review our operating costs. Bob selected Nancy as ERCOT's officer on point for the effort. After all, Bob thought, this is a human resources issue. Nancy must have misread it as an indication that she was on Bob's succession planning list. I guess Bob's extensive experience working with human resource legal issues stimulated her misread. Things had gotten to the point that made you wonder what Nancy was thinking—it wasn't making sense. Since joining ERCOT, she did seem to be in desperate need of some kind of indication that she was playing a key role at ERCOT. She might have been thinking the review was in her sweet spot.

The way it stacked up was straight out of an episode of *The Three Stooges* (again, plus Shemp). We would now have Steve, Nancy, Ron, and Mike giving input to outside consultants on what Sam and I were doing wrong and how we could improve our performance. It was just like the episode of *The Three Stooges* called "A Plumbing We Will Go," with Larry looking to shut off the main water line by digging a huge hole in the front yard. He poked his head up out of the hole and said, "I'll find this or else."

The consultants reminded me of the "Bobs" from the movie *Office Space*. The biggest difference was that these consultants had far less street smarts or sense of humor. They had no sense of perspective. In addition, they both obviously hated their jobs.

They had a script before interviewing anybody. They needed to make a case to eliminate a "chief." I figured that their mission had to be targeted at my area. What else could they be looking for?

I was on the fence as to how to play them. It wasn't my first rodeo. Such reviews had become almost routine; they just appeared in different forms—audits, investigations, cost-cutting initiatives, internal control reviews, head-count justifications, etc., etc., etc.

I didn't like spending time on those reviews, but I understood why they were needed and why there were so many of them. With no profit-and-loss measurement or shareholder wealth objective at ERCOT, our quasi-governmental fiduciary responsibility was grounded in certain government obligations such as duty of care, duty of loyalty, duty of impartiality, duty of accountability, and duty of preserving the public trust in our operation. Compliance with such obligations could only be assessed through those reviews. Some we conducted ourselves, but, as I witnessed during my five-plus years at ERCOT, most were conducted by outsiders allegedly specializing in such reviews.

As a former accountant and CPA, I had an excellent track record for satisfying such inquiries. The attest function, more commonly referred to as auditing, was a big part of my formal training. I not only knew the drill, I knew what the outsider was looking for. I could put together a good package to meet the needs of the reviewer. My group always got high marks.

I could easily show how my group delivered—both with great people and their performance. No doubt they would be impressed with our list of accomplishments, and I could tout the efficiency and effectiveness of my highly qualified team poised for the next set of challenges.

I would produce the evidence for them: A page detailing the nature and huge volume of daily transactions under our responsibility. Another page of detailed support showing what we do to satisfy the need for accurate accounting for every one of the daily usage transactions in our $30 billion retail market.

Perhaps I would come up with another page documenting the activities of our call center and customer representatives. And another outlining the long list of market participant meetings requiring our support. We would have a final pitch showing our readiness to implement those six million-plus automated real-time usage meters still to be installed by the transmission and distribution companies. That should be enough for these "Bobs."

I just couldn't do all that again. The snub of the blackballing stakeholder groups and the whole fiduciary responsibility thing had worn me down. Not to mention the fact that I couldn't take many more ERCOT management committee meetings. There was no way I would be promoted to the new chief operating officer position. That was already a done deal.

Besides, the Public Utility Commissioners and their staff had always been good to me. They deserved an accurate report from the "Bobs." I knew my time at ERCOT was running out, so I decided to be brutally honest with them. Easy, fast, and crystal clear.

The "Bobs" said that they were on a productivity and cost-saving mission. It was an area that they said was their passion and where they had the requisite training and expertise.

The passion thing didn't hold up for me. The "Bobs" greeted me in robotic fashion. They gave me firm handshakes and made proper eye contact. Both wore glasses. They might not have needed them to see better, but they looked more competent by wearing them. Their experience was limited to consulting firms. That meant that they already had a prepared draft of their report with a list of standard recommendations for improvement. They had that look in their eyes of wanting to be somewhere else. I knew what they were thinking: "If only I could get a real job."

The "Bobs" were in cruise control mode. They followed their script of open-ended questions. They really perked up when they realized I was giving them a chance to report something more than their prepared list of standard recommendations.

It was a comfortable meeting for me. Honesty can make you feel that way. My only challenge was to be sure they left with my intended takeaway. That was the purpose of the meeting, wasn't it? They had to have my key points documented and burned into their thinking before they left the room.

I told them, "I don't have much to do day-to-day. Our major projects are either completed or on hold. My staff is world class. They work quite well on their own." I could tell that those two points got their attention as they sat up taller in their seats.

"My part of the ERCOT wholesale market overhaul project, the settlements and billing piece, has been finished for a while. There is nothing more to do there until the rest of the project is completed." They started taking notes. They disengaged their cruise control and began tapping the accelerator.

I gave them another important fact. "The project to incorporate six million-plus automated meters into our system is underway. The transmission and distribution companies have to make the purchases and phase in the installations. We can't do anything until that happens. We will then phase them into our system accordingly over the next three to five years. Honestly, my staff doesn't need me for that. The groundwork is already done. The system links are already in place. The only issue on our end is to figure out how to achieve the computing speed to handle the huge new volume of data. Hopefully, Ron, will figure that out." The "Bobs" looked at each other: "Is Ray going where we think he is going?"

"My lieutenants, Betty Day and Dale Goodman, don't need me. They can run things without my overhead. We haven't had a dispute to resolve in years. They know precisely what to do, how to do it, and how to deal with any problems that might come up."

They couldn't believe their ears. This was great! But what should they recommend?

I gave them the punchline. "I need to be promoted to the new chief operating officer position to leverage my accomplishments. Otherwise, I'll have to deal with the fact that I have worked myself out of a job."

The "Bobs" were surprised and obviously excited about the pat on the back they would get from these findings. They couldn't write fast enough, trying not to show their excitement. When they finished, they thanked me for my time. For the first time in the meeting, they looked alive and happy. It was pathetic.

I left no chance for them to screw up their assignment. My job should be eliminated. The Public Utility Commissioners would get an honest report on my activities. The skids were adequately greased. As a bonus, the Three Stooges, plus Shemp, would be pleased.

48

One Last Warning

December 2007 brought its usual holiday festivities and the all-too-familiar ERCOT drama. Sue and I enjoyed the festival of lights presented by the neighborhood on and around Thirty-Seventh Street and Guadalupe near downtown Austin. We had the kids in town for Christmas. The wind chill made it seem a lot cooler than historic normal temperatures. No golf or leisurely walks outside, and we needed to bundle up to go out to eat. I wanted to be sure that our kids saw all the sights around Austin. I thought it was probably our last Christmas with ERCOT.

Ron threw a holiday party at his house. His new Olympic-sized swimming pool was finally completed, although we couldn't go out to get a closer look because it was so cold. It had night lights strategically placed around its edges. The large glass door facing the pool gave the house a resort feeling. Bob Kahn was really impressed with the size of the house and just had to show his wife the upstairs media room. This was what she should expect to see in the house of a highly qualified chief information officer.

In addition to the swimming pool and media room, the house was full of beautiful furnishings. For a brief moment, I wondered if Ron had taken a page out of the Ken Shoquist book on fraud. Probably not. I didn't see Ron nearly as smart as Ken. He was a borrow-and-spend guy, just like his approach to the ERCOT wholesale market overhaul project.

To start the new year, Bob began interviewing candidates for the new chief operating officer position. It was a short list that included the two marquee candidates. Trip Doggett, the stakeholder darling candidate, would be the pick. Bob had to interview me for the optics. The unaffiliated board members and Public Utility Commissioners would need to know that he interviewed me. Trip would be a home run for Bob, but he did need to interview me. No need for him to miss touching third base on his way to home plate.

My interview with Bob was great. We both knew the planned outcome, but we took the opportunity to put all our cards on the table. Bob had the winning hand. We only needed to discuss how it would play out.

Bob's first question was to ask me what I thought was the most pressing issue for the new chief operating officer.

"That's easy," I said. "Get the ERCOT wholesale market overhaul project finished sooner rather than later. The new estimate will likely exceed $300 million. That calls for a renewed sense of urgency and focus, don't you think, Bob?"

Bob didn't respond right away. He let me complete my thought. I issued my last warning: "We can't be derelict in our financial responsibility. If we don't show how we will get it finished quickly, we'll all be fired."

Bob was prepared for the warning. It was exactly what he expected. His response was equally predictable. Bob said, "That's not our problem. The stakeholders and their process will take care of that. We just need to continue to facilitate that effort and focus on cutting costs related to our day-to-day operations."

It was all going according to Hoyle. I knew what I had to do.

I said, "I understand. You know a helluva lot more about the legislative, regulatory, and stakeholder environments than I do. It's just my nature as an officer to feel a sense of fiduciary responsibility for the clusterfuck out there. I really can't stand on the sideline anymore, and I refuse to be sucked in as one of the clowns in that three-ring circus."

Bob was calm. He still hadn't heard anything he hadn't anticipated. He had prepared for my indignation.

My next move surprised him. He didn't know that the communication from the "Bobs" was part of my plan. I said, "I want to contribute to your ERCOT cost-cutting efforts—give me a couple of months. If I can't find another job, let me go with a fair severance agreement."

Bob was a little surprised at my preemptive strike, but I think he genuinely appreciated my proposal for the way out. It was clean, crisp, and fair—just what he wanted. Ultimately the proposal was a win-win in what could have resulted in an ugly divorce. Bob was a human resources lawyer. He knew what to do. He would give me a couple of months.

Bob hired Trip as the new chief operating officer. He was indeed the quintessential stakeholder darling—the consultant who was the leader of the one-year-plus effort of TNT to decide on new protocols and a leader of the stakeholder transition effort of TPTF that brought the ERCOT wholesale market overhaul project to its current estimate of more than $300 million to complete. He had been the unanimous pick of stakeholders and Bob's only choice. It was like putting the band back together for more good times of peace, love, and the ERCOT wholesale market overhaul project for the good of Texas consumers.

In all fairness to Trip, a big reason why he was a stakeholder darling was because he did have the qualifications to manage the ERCOT operations. I had no complaints about the pick. Trip and I always got along, and he was the right fit for ERCOT's ongoing operations. He even reached out to me to discuss how I might stay on board. That wasn't going to happen, but it was a nice gesture.

The only problem with selection of Trip as the new ERCOT chief operating officer was that it was now a certainty that the ERCOT wholesale market overhaul project would fail. The original manager of the project, Kathy Hager, was on the right track. Someone had to get the stakeholders to cave in and commit to end the project one way or another. That someone would not be our new chief operating officer. Bringing in the leader of TNT and TPTF efforts was a good indicator that he wasn't going to do anything to press stakeholders to complete the project.

Kathy's replacement was still stumbling around. "Lou Costello" never did get Ron to explain to him "What's on second?" He complained to me that Ron wouldn't tell him "Who was on first," so he thought he would move on to his second question to see if that would give him any insights into the answer to his first question. Just kidding, of course, but I was glad I would never have to have ERCOT business discussions with him again.

All the officers met in management committee to discuss the "Bobs'" consulting project. The Three Stooges plus Shemp were obviously excited about the result. We didn't discuss any details. Bob said that the job was completed and the Public Utility Commission was reviewing their recommendations. We would get the results soon.

After the meeting, Bob caught up with me. He handed me an ERCOT pin. It was a five-year service pin that he was obligated to give to me. There was no presentation in front of the management team or, better yet, at a lunch and learn, with a thank you for a job well done. Just a trinket he had to give me. I was sure not to let the door hit me in the ass when I left the meeting room.

Within a week after that, my job was eliminated. There was no place for me anymore at ERCOT.

Within a month after my departure, the rumor mill pegged the new cost estimate for the ERCOT wholesale market overhaul project at more than $600 million. Apparently, stakeholders didn't care. Their process would take care of that. Only the best for Texas consumers.

Unlike Bob, the chairman of the Public Utility Commission did care. A little more than two months after my job was eliminated, Bob was fired, Ron was fired, and Lou Costello was fired. Mike, ERCOT's fifth in-house attorney during my tenure, and Steve avoided the axe by moving on to new jobs. And my dear friend Nancy Capezzuti, the vice president of human resources, was fired.

Trip was promoted to chief executive officer. He was instructed to stay clear of the ERCOT wholesale market project and to hire a new chief operating officer selected by the chairman of the Public Utility Commission. The new chief operating officer was put in charge of completing the ERCOT wholesale market overhaul project within six months. He was freed from any Stakeholders' Golden Rule nonsense. The stakeholders and ERCOT staff were instructed to do whatever he told them to do. The chairman of the Public Utility Commission just wanted the damn thing done. The new chief operating officer had previously implemented two similar projects to completion. He would get it done.

I never spoke with Bob after my departure. I wondered if he, like good old Tom Noel, would tell me, "I should have listened to you."

It probably didn't bother Bob too much. A trip to the poker room at The Venetian in Las Vegas would ease his pain. He obviously didn't know as much about the legislative and regulatory environments as either one of us had thought he did. He did know the stakeholder environment. Some stakeholder company would surely give him another chance.

For five and a half years I worked for and with people that never got it. "It's easy," they would say. "We are quasi-governmental. The stakeholders are in control. We must abide by the Stakeholders' Golden Rule to achieve our goal of outcomes in The best interest of the people of Texas. You only have to do what you are told to do."

They found out that it wasn't so easy. It was all about fraud and dereliction of duty—and something called fiduciary responsibility: A time-tested foundational concept of American business that got ignored instead of properly translated into The Stakeholders' Golden Rule and the ERCOT quasi-governmental environment.

EPILOGUE

Spiders and Snakes

There was no announcement of my departure, no public thank you for my service. I didn't expect it. Any such gesture would have been insincere. Everybody knew that a lot of stakeholders were happy to see me leave. There was no need to confuse the issue.

During my two weeks' notice period, I was permitted to attend one last board of directors meeting. My departure was never brought up. They already knew I was leaving. Bob had waited until the closed session right before the board meeting to inform them. I was never really at odds with any of the board members, except those from the independent generator group and the energy marketer group. My final interface with them was a bit awkward. Many seemed surprised and sorry to see me go. At a minimum, I was always a source of entertainment, honesty, and street smarts.

I did get one unexpected takeaway that made it all worthwhile. Miguel Espinoza, the unaffiliated board member who had led the special investigation committee, greeted me warmly, shook my hand, and made sure he made eye contact. He said, "Please know, Ray, that you really made a difference." That was enough for me. I was good to go.

Sue and I enjoyed living in Austin. Sue had a lot of friends at the school where she substituted almost every day. We both reveled in the scenery. We loved the cross section of restaurants. It was fun to be outdoors so much. It was a great place for all of that.

We loved our home. Sue had turned it into our dream home, even though it had too much space and too many rooms—pretty much standard Texas design. We would miss it too. Our last big digs. Everybody should live in a house that is too big for them at least for a few years. It will cure you of any pangs of house envy during your retirement.

We had hoped for a longer stay at ERCOT, but it was not to be. That was okay, too, though our departure felt a little unfair. Sue wouldn't let me go there. She helped me clean the tar and feathers off of my clothing. I was pleased with the man in the mirror. Fighting for what I thought was right was satisfying. I had no regrets.

As was the case with a lot of baby boomers, we found ourselves unofficially retired. Generation X was well-positioned and chomping at the bit to kick us out. We had acted the same way in our late twenties. "Experience? Experience? We don't need no stinkin' experience!" we would say.

Sue could still teach anywhere, but my options were slim to none. Obviously, I was too cynical, sarcastic, and unpredictable for a chief executive officer or board of directors position. Too unyielding for a lesser officer-level position. Too tired of trying to fit in with the politics at any executive level. Too young to collect Social Security and Medicare. My only work path forward was as a consultant. I'd worry about that later.

Sue and I weren't sure what we would do, but we knew whatever it was would probably be fun. There would be plenty of sightseeing adventures and trips to Vegas. We knew we would be happy enough doing it together. Our nest egg was modest but adequate. We accepted the possibility that we might need to spend all of it to enjoy retirement. As my grandfather once told me, "Always remember that the last suit you will ever wear won't have any pockets!"

We packed up and headed for our new home in Nashville. Our son and one of our daughters lived there. Our other daughter was not too far away in Auburn, Alabama. No grandchildren yet, but we hoped we would have some soon. We were a close family. The logistics would be much better for us in Nashville.

We would miss Austin. We rode north on the expressway toward Dallas. I turned up the seventies music playing on the radio.

The Jim Stafford song "Spiders and Snakes" (songwriters David Bellamy and Jim Stafford) brought back one of our most-cherished memories. We reminisced about Sue's two-day visit with me in Palo Alto just before the summer break in 1974, between my first and second years of graduate school.

The first day, we drove west toward the ocean on the winding road up and around the hills through the forest of giant redwoods. It was all new and fascinating for Sue. She was in "Wow!" mode the whole way.